GW01553271

LITTLE
SHIPS
of
New
Zealand

LITTLE SHIPS
of New Zealand

PAUL TITCHENER

A. H. & A. W. REED
Wellington • Sydney • London

First published 1978

A.H. & A.W. REED LTD

65-67 Taranaki Street, Wellington
53 Myoora Road, Terrey Hills, Sydney 2084
11 Southampton Row, London, WC1B 5HA
also
16-18 Beresford Street, Auckland
Cnr Mowbray & Thackeray Streets,
Waltham, Christchurch 2

© 1978 Paul Titchener

All rights reserved. No part of this publication may be re-
produced, stored in a retrieval system or transmitted in any
form or by any means electronic, mechanical, photocopying,
recording or otherwise without the prior permission of the
publishers.

ISBN 0 589 01068 9

Jacket design by Julius Petro
Typography and layout by Kevin Woolcott
Typeset by Printset Processes (1973) Ltd.
Printed by Dai Nippon Printing Co (Hong Kong) Ltd.

To the pioneer New Zealand yachtsmen and builders
who laid the foundation of a great sport

For Scott, Edward, Michael and Jane

Contents

Acknowledgments

The author is grateful to the following sources for photographs used in this book:

North Shore Times Advertiser, Takapuna, Auckland
Sea Spray, Auckland
Don Buick Photography, Auckland
Royal New Zealand Navy
Serrom Studios, Auckland
J. M. D'ath, Auckland
J. E. Farrelly, Auckland
Evening Post, Wellington
D. Forster, Switzerland
Auckland Institute and Museum
Sir Bryan Todd

Prologue

Early in 1975 the publishers approached me about the possibility of writing a fourth edition of Ronald Carter's *Little Ships*. Three editions of this book were published in the 1940s, the last in 1948.

The prospect, quite frankly, frightened me. First, as a child growing up on the shores of the Waitemata Harbour I had read and reread *Little Ships* until I could virtually quote whole chapters verbatim. To take up the story of New Zealand yachting where Ronald Carter had stopped was, I thought, beyond my capabilities. Secondly, the fantastic growth of New Zealand yachting in the three decades since 1948 meant that it would require more time and effort than I thought I could devote, on a part-time basis.

But with these misgivings I decided to take up the challenge. As I got deeper into the necessary research before one word was even written, I realised that here was a great story to be written. But what worried me was whether I could follow in Ronald Carter's footsteps and do justice to the great New Zealand sport of yachting.

Late in 1975 I entered into correspondence with Ronald Carter, now a very elderly man living in Remuera, Auckland. He greatly encouraged me. As any author knows, there are times when one feels it is all a waste of time, and Mr Carter's encouragement came right at the time I needed it.

Little Ships of New Zealand (Ronald Carter did not want the name of his classic book used again) is now completed, and I hereby acknowledge the debt I owe to Mr Carter — not only for his encouragement but also for his permission to quote freely from *Little Ships*.

Readers of *Little Ships of New Zealand* will no doubt wonder how much of Ronald Carter's original *Little Ships* is in this new volume.

Originally the intention was merely to update *Little Ships* to the end of 1976, but the deeper I researched the subject the more I realised that with the passing of time further information on the pioneer boatbuilders and on yachting in general had become available. Therefore only one chapter — on the ill-fated *Strathcona* — remains as Ronald Carter originally wrote it. Even this chapter has been updated. Every other chapter has had amendments made and additional information inserted. And of course anything relating to the great sport of yachting since 1948 (the date of the last edition of *Little Ships*) is entirely my own work.

Lastly I owe to my wife Prue a great deal of thanks for her encouragement at critical times, for her typing of the manuscript from my notes and at all times for her objective criticism.

Bayswater, Auckland
Goodwood, Hamilton

Paul Titchener
January 1977

1.

The Auckland Anniversary Regatta

THE HISTORY OF New Zealand yachting can be traced back to 15 September 1840, when the ship *Anna Watson* arrived in the Waitemata Harbour with officials who were to lay out the site of the proposed capital city. These officials included Lieutenant Governor Hobson, the Surveyor-General Felton Matthew and their respective staffs.

The *Anna Watson* dropped anchor off a headland (which was to be later named Point Britomart, now virtually completely removed by harbour reclamations in the early part of this century) and the official party proceeded ashore to complete negotiations for the acquisition of the site of the new city with the Maori owners. These negotiations were completed satisfactorily, and on 18 September 1840 the flag was hoisted on the headland to signal the purchase of the site for the capital city. The event was saluted by the *Anna Watson* with 21 guns. This was followed by a salute of 15 guns by the other vessel in the harbour, the barque *Platina*. The *Anna Watson* then fired a seven-gun salute in honour of Governor Hobson, which was responded to by those on shore with three hearty cheers and "one cheer more".

To celebrate formally the historic occasion a regatta was held in the afternoon. This regatta is the first recorded organised yachting event in the history of New Zealand (although it is possible that sailing and rowing races for wagers had occurred between crews of naval vessels lying in the Bay of Islands, and merchant, whaling or sealing ships in harbours in both the North and South Islands at an earlier date). Records of such events do not exist, and the regatta on the Auckland harbour on September 18 1840 must be regarded as the first sailing and rowing event in New Zealand.

The programme on this day consisted of three events. A five-oared gig belonging to the Surveyor-General was matched against a six-oared gig from the *Anna Watson* over a course of 3.2 km (2 miles). The extra oar in the *Anna Watson's* crew must have proved beneficial for this crew won handsomely. The next event was a sailing whaleboat race for a prize of £5, and the final event was a race between two Maori war canoes.

From this three-event regatta was to grow the sport of yachting in New Zealand. It has always been dominated by Auckland, because of the magnificent Hauraki Gulf and its kindly climate. It is interesting to relate that in a despatch from Russell on 10 November 1840 Hobson states that he had just returned from a visit to the Waitemata where "I found the officers of the Government, the mechanics, and labourers, under their orders, proceeding with the necessary works for establishing the town which I contemplate being the future seat of Government and which I propose distinguishing by the name of Auckland."

In March 1841 Captain Hobson took up official residence in Auckland, and on 3 May 1841 New Zealand was proclaimed independent of New South Wales. Hobson became Governor instead of Lieutenant Governor. In 1842 the Imperial Government officially recognised Auckland as the capital of New Zealand, much to the disappointment of the New Zealand Land Company at Port Nicholson (Wellington).

The early settlers of Auckland decided to continue the regatta to celebrate the founding of the city each Anniversary day, which falls each 29 January. This tradition has continued to the present day, and the Auckland Anniversary Regatta is proudly called the biggest one-day regatta in the world. All commercial shipping ceases, and the harbour is a mass of sails and motor boats. Every available vantage position

A common type from early regattas. The scow *Thistle*, typical of the workhorses of the Auckland province before being replaced by the motor truck.

Auckland regatta 1912. The trading cutter *Sunderland* with full sail set (including a water-sail under the main boom).

Regatta Day 1908. The scow *Havoc* with "a bone in her teeth", running before a brisk southerly in Rangitoto Channel.

on the many headlands around the harbour is packed with spectators.

However it was not always this way. In the very early days of the 1840s and 1850s the greatest interest centred around the trading vessels, for these craft made up the bulk of the racing fleet. These trading vessels were the life-blood of early New Zealand, as roading was non-existent and each little port or coastal inlet was serviced by these sailing vessels. However on that one day in January every master made sure his vessel was in Auckland for the regatta. The ships were slipped and bottoms scraped for all possible speed, as the races were sailed with intense keenness (not only for the prizes offered but also for the heavy wagers made between competing captains and crews). The public also bet heavily on the favourites in the various races.

It is interesting to examine the gradual transition of the racing fleets from trading vessels to pleasure boats. This transition was hastened in the last quarter of the nineteenth century by the rapid increase in the building of steam-propelled vessels and the resulting demise of sailing craft. The finest fleet of sail trading vessels, whether they be schooner, ketch, or cutter rigged, was in the 1880 regatta, where the fleet raced for a prize of £100 and the master's prize of a sextant. The main race drew an entry of 12 vessels, including the schooners *Amy Wilson* and *Sybil*, both newly launched sister ships designed and built by the shipbuilding genius James Barbour at Aratapu, up the Northern Wairoa River. The schooners, each of 150 tonnes, were fast sailors and the great favourites.

The rest of the fleet, consisting of the *Transit, Borealis, Caledonia, Reward, May Anderson, Fleetwing, Adaah, Mazeppa, Ryno,* and *Albatross* (winner of the Lyttelton regatta), made a magnificent sight as they squared away for the race of approximately 64 km round Tiri Tiri Island. The *Mazeppa*, which had built up a notable reputation in her fast ocean passages to the islands, was looked upon by some as an easy winner, but she came nowhere, tailing the fleet home. Captain McKenzie's *Borealis* was also thought to be a likely winner, but as she was brigantine rigged she was not heavily supported because no brigantine had previously won an Auckland regatta. She eventually came fourth. Another great favourite in the race was the *Transit*, captained by that famous racing skipper Mat Hooper.

What an inspiring sight these 12 ocean-going

sailing vessels must have made as they raced neck and neck out round North Head, and how intense the excitement must have been as the watching spy-glasses picked out the first vessel to round Tiri Tiri Island. Soon the leaders were roaring up the channel with a bone in their teeth. The final placings in this most exciting race: *Sybil* first, *Amy Wilson* second, *Transit* third. As the *Sybil* was allowing the *Transit* a time al-

A fine example of the kind of trading vessel now extinct. The trading ketch *Endeavour* in the trading vessels race, 1919.

lowance of seven minutes, the latter vessel was placed first on handicap.

The second race for big cutters, also round Tiri Tiri, resulted in the *Rangatira* never being challenged and beating *The Sovereign of the Seas* by three minutes.

The third race for yachts under six tonnes drew out 12 starters, and was won by the famous *Jessie Logan*, winner in her class for a number of years. In the fourth race for small cutters, seven boats crossed the starting line. After a great tussle between the *Henry* and *Toz*, the former just managed to get the gun.

The fifth race, which was for open boats, was won by *Toz*, with *Albert* second. The sixth and last race, for "big yachts", was won by the *Thetis*; but just what is meant by "big yachts" is not made clear in the records which survive.

A summary of this regatta programme discloses the fact that about 20 trading vessels,

represented by schooners and cutters, along with perhaps 25 yachts, composed the entire regatta fleet of 98 years ago. In spite of their lack in numbers, however, they made a very brave sight. We who come after must give a thought to the skippers and crews who raced with such keenness in the trading vessel matches of long ago, for they undoubtedly assisted very materially in keeping alive the spirit of the Auckland Anniversary Regattas.

What great changes time has wrought since 1880. Auckland was then just a modest town of 27,423 inhabitants, perched on the edge of rising back country. Today the whole Auckland isthmus is a bustling metropolis approaching a million people. These intrepid early settlers would not recognise their rather sleepy coastal town and port. This small population was not sufficient to support a costly fleet of racing yachts, although by 1852 a yacht club grandly named the Auckland Yacht Club had been founded. Little is known of this club, the first in New Zealand, although in an issue of 21

The scows *Gannet* and *Seagull* running past Rangitoto light. Regatta Day 1905.

An early regatta keeler. The *Yum Yum* was built in 1887 and is still afloat.

A straight stem yawl sailing up Auckland harbour in 1902. Like other early regatta racers she was also used for fishing and carrying cargo.

December 1852 the leading paper of the day, the *Southern Cross*, carried an advertisement calling for a special general meeting of the club "for the purpose of closing the business of the 1851-52 season, electing new officers and committee and taking steps for promoting the forthcoming regatta". No other information concerning this club exists, except for a 16-page booklet dated 1859 listing club laws and membership; it is held in the Auckland Public Library. It would appear that this club existed solely for the purpose of promoting the Auckland Anniversary Regattas.

Then in 1871, following the anniversary regatta prize-giving for that year, a group of prize-winners and other keen yachtsmen met outside the Thames Hotel (now the site of the Dilworth Building in Customs Street). Under the flickering light of a gas lamp they re-founded the Auckland Yacht Club. The club prospered, and in 1887 absorbed another club, the Hauraki Yacht Club.

In 1901 it was decided to rename the club, rather grandly, the New Zealand Yacht Squadron. In 1902 the Yacht Squadron, as it was called around the waterfront, received two major accolades. The British Admiralty granted the 20 yachts on the club register the right to fly the Blue Ensign undefaced, and the Secretary of State for the Colonies in London granted the squadron the Royal prefix. The club which started under a gas light outside a hotel 30 years before, became the Royal New Zealand Yacht Squadron.

Other yacht clubs were being established in Auckland. The Parnell Sailing Club was founded in 1884, although all records of this club have been lost. In 1882 there had been a breakaway from the Auckland Yacht Club; it was named the Waitemata Yacht Club, membership being confined solely "to those who own or are interested in a yacht". This restriction was apparently aimed at those "social" yachtsmen who joined the Auckland Yacht Club but did not get their feet wet. After discussion between the two clubs in 1887 the breakaway group rejoined the Auckland Yacht Club and the Waitemata Yacht Club was allowed to lapse.

As the population of Auckland continued to grow and prosper, the number of yachts also increased and other yacht clubs were formed. Of particular importance was the establishment of the North Shore Sailing Club in 1894. Devonport, on the northern shore of the Waitemata Harbour, was an important yacht and shipbuilding centre, with such famous boatbuilders as Robert Logan and Charles Bailey having their yards in the area. The first regatta to be held on the north side of the Waitemata Harbour was held on 9 November 1881, and it is surprising that a club was not formed before 1894. The initial meeting of the North Shore Sailing Club was held in the Devonport Borough Council Chambers in September 1894, and Mr Alex Alison was elected the first commodore. The club promoted three regattas each season, and sponsored "a class of yachts about

The cutter *Pastime* (1105), a veteran of countless regatta races. The author believes *Pastime* is the oldest yacht still sailing in New Zealand.

26 feet keel, or centreboard" which came to be known in derogatory fashion as the "class for hacks". Nonetheless it proved very popular with the yachtsmen of the day.

In 1901 the name of the club was changed to the North Shore Yacht Club. It retained this name until 1921, when it was again changed, this time to the Akarana Yacht Club (Akarana being the Maori name for Auckland). This change of name preceded a change of venue; in 1922 it was decided to move the club from Devonport to the southern shore of the Waitemata, because nearly all the officers and members of the club lived on that side of the harbour. The new clubhouse was established in a building near Campbells Point, but with the reclamation of Mechanics Bay during World War II the club was again forced to move, this time to its present location in Okahu Bay, in 1946. In February 1937 the Akarana Yacht Club was honoured by the King when he approved the royal warrant to the club, which then became the Royal Akarana Yacht Club. Club members were allowed to fly the Blue Ensign of the Royal Navy Reserve defaced with the club's badge (a Maori sailing canoe).

This club became only the third yacht club in New Zealand to have the royal prefix, the other two being the Royal New Zealand Yacht Squadron (also in Auckland) and the Royal Port Nicholson Yacht Club in Wellington.

The North Shore Yacht Club also gave birth to another of Auckland's senior yacht clubs, the Devonport Yacht Club, which was formed by a breakaway group of Devonport yachtsmen at a meeting held immediately after the annual general meeting of the North Shore Yacht Club in August 1905. This meeting was held in Mr W. H. Oliver's garden shed at the back of his house in Anne Street, Devonport. Mr G. B. Graham, who owned the yacht *Daisy*, was elected commodore, and members decided to adopt the Red Ensign of the Mercantile Marine as the club ensign and the flag "F" of the international code as the club pennant. The flag "F" is a red pennant with a white cross vertical and horizontal, with the addition of the Southern Cross in the inner upper quadrant.

These four pioneer yacht clubs ushered Auckland yachting into the twentieth century.

What a difference the yachting scene is in the last quarter of the century compared with those early days: from a total of two gigs, three whaleboats and two Maori war canoes in the first regatta held on the harbour in 1840 to celebrate the founding of Auckland, to the 1976 regatta with well over 1000 yachts ranging from 2 m to 20 m long, in 31 different classes.

In the past 136 years the annual regatta has been cancelled only once, in 1900 during the Boer War. Two world wars, several other wars such as Korea and Vietnam, economic depressions in the late 1880s and in the early 1930s, gales and other natural phenomena, have not stopped the Auckland Anniversary Regatta, so proudly titled the "largest one-day regatta in the world".

Auckland Anniversary Regatta racing in later years. *Waione* (A33), in her modern Bermuda rig, and *Tuahine* (A6) hard on the wind just after a start in 1964. Ian Titchener at the *Waione's* helm.

2.

The kauri pine

THE MAGNIFICENT KAURI TREE, known to botanists as *Agathis australis*, grows only in the northern half of the North Island. It can be rightly described as the prince of boatbuilding timbers. For both house and boatbuilding it is unsurpassed by any other timber found in New Zealand; in fact it would be difficult to find a better wood anywhere else in the world. This is a bold statement, but it reflects the words of the boatbuilders themselves, many of whom have worked with teak and mahogany, classed A1 to Lloyd's highest specifications, with English oak and New Zealand kauri running a close third.

It has always been felt that if New Zealand kauri could be obtained in limitless quantities and at a reasonable price it would eventually become universal as a boatbuilding timber throughout the world. Of course this will never eventuate because the isolated position of New Zealand and the consequent heavy freightage over long distances mean that it is not profitable for countries on the other side of the world to import the timber in any great quantity.

A little has found its way to England. The British Navy used it for certain parts of its ships, and on occasions some English yachts have had their decks laid in kauri pine. But apart from this, the wood is almost unknown on the other side of the world. On the other hand Australia, our nearest neighbour in commerce, has been using our kauri for over a century, millions of metres having been shipped over during this period. In addition to this, New Zealanders themselves have made great inroads on the kauri forests for house and boatbuilding, the consequence being that the supply is falling off in an alarming manner.

This is most unfortunate, because practically no attempts have been made to replace the mighty kauri forests which once covered the whole of the northern areas of the North Island. The day does not seem far distant when kauri timber will no longer be obtainable even in small quantities.

A most valuable by-product of the kauri tree is the kauri gum, the basis of some of the finest of the world's varnishes. Seventy years ago, thousands of gum-diggers were occupied in exploiting the precious kauri gum, buried at varying distances under the surface of the ground. They dug over large tracts of what is now known as the gum lands, or poor lands, of North Auckland Province, earning as much as $170 a tonne for good clear gum.

At one time — nobody knows how long ago — giant kauri trees grew where the gum-diggers worked, but within living memory there have been no trees standing in these areas. The only evidence we have that a mighty forest did once occupy these lands is found in the trunks and stumps of old trees, often buried many metres under the ground. How the forests became extinct nobody seems to know, although some say that they were fired by the early Maoris. A typical example of one of the old northern gumfields is the Northland farming district of Mangawai, which today shows little evidence of the former mighty kauri forest that once stood there.

Today the kauri gum industry is finished. Most of the gum has been dug out, and large areas of virgin country in Northland, once covered with kauri forests, have been converted into dairy farms. The only tracts of kauri forest of any extent are under the protection of the New Zealand Government, which now guards them with the utmost caution.

A kauri tree a thousand or so years old is a veritable giant, of magnificent appearance. Towering straight as a knife blade into the air, the tree is clear of branches for the greater portion of its height. Only near the top will be seen the tufts of branches and foliage; for the rest, the bole is one long unbroken length of mottled grey-green bark.

The wood varies in colour, but broadly

speaking the sap is of a whitish hue against the darker cream colour of the heart. It is a fine timber to work, a boatbuilder once describing it as being a "kindly" wood; this description sums it up admirably, for it does take kindly to the plane and saw, nails and screws.

Newly seasoned, the wood is easy to work, because owing to its straight grain and absence of knots, it planes and saws well. It hardens considerably with age, and alters colour to a light brownish hue. But perhaps one of its greatest virtues is its elasticity, for it will take a carefully driven nail almost at the end of the grain without splitting. It steams well, and will bend or twist to an astonishing degree. Last, but by no means least, the wood holds well any paint, oil or varnish that is applied to its surface. So here in New Zealand one might say we have the perfect boatbuilding timber, except for one very small fault: no matter how long kauri has been seasoned, it will under trying conditions of very dry and wet weather, continue to "move" slightly.

Today all the available kauri comes from very carefully controlled thinnings from the Government-owned kauri forests, now national parks in the central Northland region. All the forests of Great Barrier Island and Coromandel are completely worked out, apart from the odd tree still standing, left by the ruthless bushman because its inaccessibility or physical defects rendered it unprofitable for milling. This shortage is reflected in the price of boatbuilding kauri. In the mid 1970s the price is some 50 times the price at the turn of the century.

The majority of the traditionally built New Zealand yachts, (that is, built prior to the advent of marine grade plywood) had double skinned decks, the under-skin being diagonal planked, overlaid with "fore and aft" deck planking. In spite of careful caulking and seam filling, the decks tended to open very slightly in very hot weather. Old-time yachtsmen used to say of certain yachts that it was dangerous to sit on the deck when putting about, because the movement of the decks could pinch one's bottom. It was necessary to throw onto the other tack so that one's bottom could be released!

Other evidence of this slight timber movement can be usually found on examining the plank ends fastened around a square or tuck-sterned yacht or launch. This movement is so slight as to be of no consequence. However it is a different story when a single-skin kauri-

Shipwright shaping pohutukawa knees at Bailey and Lowes's yard in 1905.

planked vessel is hauled out of the water for an extended period. As the planking dries and the timber shrinks, the movement can place strain on the fastenings. It also allows the caulking to dry and crack. Once back in the water, however, the timber again swells and the vessel is "tight" once again. This "tightening" period usually takes about 60 hours, and considerable water can be made through the opened seams in this time. Oldtimers always rubbed soap into the seams to prevent this leakage, the soap of course being squeezed out as the seams closed.

This timber movement is the only fault in an otherwise perfect boatbuilding wood. As to its lasting qualities, kauri-built yachts are still afloat, in some cases 85 years after they were launched. Examples of such yachts are the Logan-built cutters *Moana* and *Mahaki*, both built before the turn of the century and both still sound and sailing regularly.

In the early days of New Zealand yacht-building, boatbuilders, following the custom of the mother country, naturally looked about for a hardwood suitable for holding the kauri hulls together, for we have no English oak to draw upon. Their choice rested mainly on the pohutukawa, what is more popularly known as the

Christmas tree. The tree grows all round the coastline of the North Island, usually right at the cliff edges, hanging most tenaciously to crumbling precipices yet seldom falling into the sea. It is a twisty, gnarled tree, with finely curved roots and branches admirably suited to the boatbuilder requiring stems, knees and floors. It is in every way a hardwood of the first order.

Yet there is a strange thing about the wood of the pohutukawa. Although its natural birthplace is found wherever salt spray can reach its roots, it has been proved when pulling old boats to pieces that whereas the kauri pine planking is still sound even after 50 years, the pohutukawa stems and knees have become soft and pithy, with no natural strength remaining. In some cases they have simply rotted away. It is a good wood, with amazing strength, but it just cannot outlast kauri. So today, wherever practicable, boatbuilders are putting in kauri stems, built up and strengthened from two to three pieces depending on the shape of the stem.

Puriri is another native hardwood used in boat construction in the same manner as pohutukawa. It is also very tough, but has not been used to the same extent.

For single-skinned yachts, a variety of different woods are used for inside timbering. New Zealand mangeao and Southland beech (also known as silver beech), as well as Australian spotted gum, are perhaps the most popular, although Canadian birch has also been used extensively. However after a good deal of experimenting it has been found that the Australian spotted gum takes a lot of beating, and it is used extensively by boatbuilders in New Zealand today.

Iron fastenings throughout a pleasure vessel's hull have never been tolerated by New Zealand yachtsmen. They ask: "Why put in wood to last a hundred years, and fastenings which may or may not go long before that time?" So although it has been proved in other countries that good iron fastenings do last a long time, the average New Zealand yachtsman wants his boatbuilder to do as his father did before him. His father's yachts were not iron-fastened, and many are still

The frames of the scow *Vesper* set up in 1904. Note the steam-bent timbers, flat floors and centreboard slot. Bailey and Lowes's yard.

The kind of pretty trading ketch which established Auckland as a major shipbuilding centre at the turn of the century.

staunch vessels today. This prejudice against iron may be in some cases just an old-fashioned idea, but New Zealand boatbuilders still believe there is no better fastening than the "yellow metal". So we use copper nails and brass and bronze screws, bolts, dumps, tie-bars, keel bolts and chainplates. In the more expensive jobs, all deck hardware is of yellow metal or stainless steel. So beside having good wood, New Zealand yachts are also well fastened. They are naturally also usually highly priced.

As Ronald Carter wrote 30 years ago: "So now the truth is out; we possess a mighty fine fleet of pleasure yachts, but they have been well paid for!"

Broadly speaking, a lead keel cutter or sloop, built on the three-skin diagonal principle of construction with first class workmanship and materials and fitted with all the latest electronic sailing aids would cost about $7000 a metre. A 9 m half-tonner built on the traditional pattern could represent an outlay of nearly $70,000. The cost of materials — not of labour — would be the greatest cost factor in such a boat. The days of the "one-off" design, as has been the case in New Zealand yachting for the past 100 years, are therefore numbered. Following world trends,

the factory concept of mass-produced stock designs is inevitable if the price of boats is not to rise so high that only the very wealthy can afford the sport.

This is a regrettable but inevitable trend as the old-time craftsman is replaced by a production line worker in a factory similar to a vehicle assembly plant. Modern synthetic materials such as fibreglass, ferro-cement and plastic are today commonplace, and even the most traditional of classes, the 6.7 m (22 ft) mullet boats, are now built in fibreglass off a common mould.

Yet all these increasing costs seem to have made no difference to Auckland's (and indeed all New Zealand's) yacht and power boatbuilding boom. This boom started after World War II — firstly by amateur builders, mostly returned servicemen. The momentum has carried on, perhaps faster each year, to the stage where today in Auckland a new boat, either power or sail, over 9 m is launched each day. The problem now created is where to park these boats because marinas and mooring areas are full. It would appear that money is more plentiful than water.

If this rate of building continues, one cannot even visualise to what dimensions the New Zealand, and in particular the Auckland, boating fleet will have grown in the next 100 years.

3.

The Bailey family

TWO FAMILIES completely dominated New Zealand yachting for a period of 70 years from the 1870s to the 1940s, and even today their influence on yacht design and construction is still marked. These families were the Baileys and the Logans. Each family had one advantage — numerous sons to carry on the family traditions and expertise from one generation to another. The Baileys were of English stock and preceded the Logans by 30-odd years to New Zealand. The patriarch of the family, Charles Bailey, was born in Auckland in 1843, while the Logans, a Scottish family headed by the redoubtable Robert Logan, did not arrive in Auckland from the Clyde until 1874.

Both families were intense rivals, but between them they made the name of Auckland famous in the yachting world for the design and construction of fast, wholesome yachts and trading vessels. Their influence extended far beyond New Zealand shores, past Australia to South Africa and even to England and the western seaboard of the United States. This influence was felt not only in yachts but in the design and building of trading vessels — both sail and steam propelled — ferry steamers, coastal steamers, rowing skiffs and even surf boats. As this narrative is confined to yachts, the history of these two fine families will be restricted to these vessels only.

Charles Bailey was born in Auckland in 1843 of parents only recently arrived from England. His father unfortunately died soon after Charles was born, and he was raised by a stepfather. As is often the case in such a family, young Charles did not see eye to eye with his stepfather, and at the age of 12 he ran away from home and school to make his own way in the world.

His first job was as a messenger boy. He became a house painter and photographer's assistant before finding the trade that really suited him — boatbuilding. He became apprenticed to Henry Niccol, who had a shipbuilding yard at the foot of Anne Street and Garden Terrace on the Devonport foreshore. Henry Niccol had at that time the largest patent slip in Australasia, capable of handling vessels of up to 700 tonnes. The slip was manufactured in England and was used until 1879. By then the growth of Devonport and subdivision of land for housing around the slip had created agitation for the removal of the slip. Certainly its ways extended across Queens Parade, and sometimes blocked through traffic. It was taken up and sold to a company in Sydney.

Charles Bailey left the employ of Henry Niccol in 1871 and joined George Beddoes, who had opened a shipbuilding yard under North Head in 1858. In 1861 he moved the yard to the foreshore at the foot of Church Street, on the present site of the North Shore Rowing Club Shed. On this site he built a big shipwrighting shed, which was also used for local dances. George Beddoes also built the Masonic Hotel, which is still standing, in 1866. He was an enterprising shipbuilder, constructing the first composite vessel built in New Zealand. This was the ferry boat *Devonport*, built for Mr F. G. Somerfield; it had iron frames and kauri planking.

Charles Bailey was 28 years of age and a fully qualified shipwright. He was appointed yard foreman, and supervised the construction of both the *Devonport* and the 143-tonne paddle-steamer *Royal Alfred*, which was capable of 17 knots. This vessel, originally designed as a screw steamer, had the engines for the *Prince Alfred*, a 1117-tonne ship belonging to the Inter-Colonial Royal Mail Steamship Company. The launching in 1872 of this flier (which was used on the Auckland to Thames goldfield run, taking only two and three-quarter hours when pushed) was witnessed by a large crowd. The *New Zealand Herald* of the day commented that the *Royal Alfred* was "one of the finest vessels in New Zealand and a great credit to the builders

The men who created the old champions. Shipwrights employed by Charles Bailey Junior pose for the photographer in 1904.

Back-breaking work. Pitsawyers cutting the centreboard slot of the scow *Vesper*. Bailey and Lowes's yard at the turn of the century.

George Beddoes and Charles Bailey".

In 1876 George Beddoes sold the shipbuilding business to his foreman and went to live in Fiji. Bailey now had his own yard, and the genius of this man for ship and yachtbuilding quickly became apparent.

Working conditions in the 1870s were very difficult. There was no electricity and therefore none of the electrical tools we take for granted today. The only tools available were adzes, axes, planes and saws — all muscle-operated.

Today we buy timber from the mill already cut to size and planed if required. A hundred years ago it was totally different. The boat-builder bought the log just as it was when felled. He first squared the log. If planking was required, he measured the size required, drove a nail into each end of the log on the required marks, attached a chalk line, and then flicked it. The chalk line was then followed by the pit saw. This pit sawing was a laborious task. The man on top followed the chalk line while the man in

Apprentices heating pitch. The chimney stack on the right is of the Hobson Street power station, while the spire of St Patrick's church can be seen in the background.

the pit pulled and pushed the overhead saw blade. For his troubles he was covered in sawdust; and after a 12-hour day he felt he had earned his wages. Once the plank had been sawn, it had to be dressed by hand — a slow, back-breaking job.

In spite of all this primitive work (for at that stage boatbuilding had not changed for 500 years) Charles Bailey built some very gracious vessels. The majority of these vessels were island traders, ferry boats and general commercial craft — Auckland was not big enough to support a boatbuilder who specialised only in pleasure craft. Today the situation is reversed. No boat-building yard could survive by building commercial vessels alone; the pleasure boat industry is the back-bone of the trade.

The fast island schooners Fleetwing (56 tonnes), built for the Oxley brothers, and the Uli-I-Lakemba, launched in 1879, and the well known Auckland harbour ferries Victoria and Britannia established Bailey's reputation. But it was as a designer and builder of racing yachts

and gigs that he became famous throughout not only New Zealand but also Australia.

The first yacht he built was the cutter Daphne, which took to the water in 1876. This yacht proved unbeatable on the Auckland harbour; she was later bought by a Fiji yachtsman, who sailed her to Suva. Other orders for racing yachts followed. Bailey launched the Erin in 1877. It was followed by the Joy, which later went to Melbourne and as late as 1966 was still sailing on Port Phillip Bay. The Sis, a 7.3 m open yacht, was built for Mr Rory Nelson, followed by another of 7.3 m for Mr Albert Sanford called Toy. Toy won the Auckland championship, and was then sailed to Wellington where she was harbour champion. Many years later Charles Bailey Junior, Charles Senior's eldest son, put a counter on Toy while he was on a visit to Wellington. Toy was lost in a Wellington gale in 1915. Another yacht of this class was the well known Pet, which also sailed on Wellington Harbour.

Other yachts quickly followed. There was the Callipso, owned by Charles Bailey but sailed by Albert Sanford. She won the Auckland regatta in 1881, but was later wrecked on the Devonport foreshore. Others included the Tow, another

The yacht *Spray*, built by Charles Bailey in 1893, hauled out on Devonport foreshore in 1902. In the background is the Calliope dry dock.

Clinker-built dinghies of a type not seen today await buyers at Bailey and Lowes's yard in 1905.

open boat, the *Thetis* (10 tonnes), the quaintly named *Sinking Fund* (6 tonnes), later renamed *Phoenix*, *Sudden Jerk*, the *Fetulele* (23 tonnes) for Samoa, and the well known *Rangatira*, a first-class cutter.

With the growth of the business, Bailey established in 1881 another yard on the Auckland side of the harbour, while still carrying on work at the North Shore yard. This move had been brought about when Charles's eldest son Charles Junior joined the business in 1878. He commenced work as an apprentice at the age of 14 years, having resisted all efforts on his father's part to make him sit for his scholarship examination at the old Devonport School, which was pulled down in 1970. He said he was sick of school and begged to go to work on his father's beloved boats, to share with the other men the hard, rough life of the early pioneer shipbuilders. One of his first jobs was to row across the harbour in a 5.5 m whaleboat to Jagger and Parker's mill, make up a kauri log raft and tow it back to his father's yard — a man-sized job for a 14-year-old boy with only one other youth to assist him.

Charles Bailey Senior never learned the art of draughtsmanship; he always built his craft from a builder's half model. It is remarkable that he

was able to build such fast racing yachts with none of the latest scientific methods for calculating curves and areas, without which no builder would risk doing a job today.

One delightful story about Charles Senior became a legend around the Auckland waterfront at the time. He wore a long, divided beard, and was known behind his back as "Clawhammer Charlie". While inspecting a vessel under construction at his Devonport yard one day, he spotted a young apprentice making an indifferent job of caulking. "That's not the way to do it, lad," said Bailey, grabbing the caulking tools and a handful of oakum. Heavy hammer blows followed. Then the job completed, Bailey turned to walk away, only to find he was attached to the boat. In his enthusiasm to show the young apprentice how to caulk, he had hammered his beard with the oakum into the seam. It was a humble master who meekly requested his apprentice to fetch some scissors so he could be freed.

Charles Junior had been at work for only 12 months when he approached his father with the idea of trying his hand at building a small yacht. Finally gaining his parent's consent, and being warned not to waste any good timber, the young man set to work. Throughout the evening and

The famous Bailey cutter *Ida* leaving Motutapu Island, 1903.

Right: A spinnaker in stops being hoisted on *Ida* during the Auckland Anniversary Regatta in 1907. The cane hoops on the mainmast, the reefing points and the rope ties on the boom have all but disappeared from today's yachts.

A rare photograph of a now-extinct rig — a jib with yarded foot — on *Ida* in 1903. Note the sailing dress of the women.

night hours, after the hard day's work in the yard was over, young Charles, working by candle-light, constructed a very successful little racing yacht of the centre-board type, measuring 4.88 m overall.

He named his first boat *Elsie* after his favourite sister, and the yacht proved to be a champion of her class, winning races in the North Shore Regatta, the Auckland Anniversary Regatta and the Ponsonby Regatta.

Around 1881, Bailey Senior moved his yard from North Head to the city side of the harbour, setting up his business on a site just at the rear of the present-day Auckland Harbour Board building. But the position was not suitable for shipbuilding and he moved a second time. His new yard occupied the land on which the tepid swimming pool now stands. After carrying on his business for some years, he eventually re-tired, handing the yard over to the care of Charles Junior, who took his brother into part-nership. The firm then became known as C. and W. Bailey. After a few years his brother left and started a partnership in opposition known as Bailey and Lowe. Both of the original partners are now deceased, the present name of the firm being W. S. Lowe and Son.

And so, while still a comparatively young man, Charles Bailey Junior commenced build-ing what became one of the finest reputations in the Southern Hemisphere. He developed a fine reputation in the Pacific Islands, for he designed and built many fast and graceful schooners, yachts and trading cutters. He was noted for his honesty in always putting the best materials and workmanship into whatever vessel he undertook to build. Many of these craft, some well over 70 years old, are still in active service.

Today the only sign of the Bailey name left in Auckland boatbuilding is the company called Chas. Bailey and Son in Beaumont Street. But the business is owned by Mr Leo Dromgoole of the North Shore Ferry Co. and no Bailey has been associated with the company for many years.

Perhaps the most famous of all the yachts built by Charles Bailey Senior in conjunction with his son Charles Junior is the *Viking*. This fine old ship is still afloat on Wellington Har-bour. She is owned by industrialist Sir Bryan Todd, who cruises her across Cook Strait to the Sounds every year.

The *Viking* has a most interesting history.

In 1893 Mr J. L. R. Bloomfield, at that time commodore of the Royal New Zealand Yacht Squadron, placed an order with the firm for a first-class cutter, a condition being that Charles Junior should be entrusted with the task of drawing out her lines.

Charles Junior, who had learned the art of draughtsmanship, set to work and laid out a yacht measuring 19.5 m overall, 14.9 m on the waterline, 3.6 m in beam, and with 2.7 m draught of water. She was a handsome vessel, constructed in the traditional style of the period with fiddle bow, long tapered counter, deep fore-foot and moderately slack bilges. Built on the three-skin, diagonal principle, she was im-mensely strong and beautifully put together. Her black topsides, gold scroll-work, and sheer-strake ribbon and copper-sheathed underbody set her hull off perfectly in keeping with the cutter rig of that time. She carried a big spread of canvas on her main and fidded topmast, the latter being housed in hard weather. This was customary in those days when sail plans were kept low, in marked contrast to the lofty Ber-mudian-rigged cutters to today.

She was christened *Viking*, and raced suc-cessfully for many years on the Waitemata Harbour under various rigs, having had her sail plan altered from cutter to yawl and finally to the ketch rig under which she sails and oc-casionally races today. The *Viking* was owned for many years by Sir Ernest Davis, who always took a great pride in his old ship, the con-sequence being that in spite of her 83 years she is still in a wonderfully sound condition.

When Sir Ernest purchased the 24 m auxiliary schooner yacht *Morewa* a few years ago, he very kindly made a present of his beloved *Viking* to the Royal New Zealand Navy. It was a very fine gesture on Sir Ernest's part, one greatly ap-preciated by the naval authorities. The old ship was used for training officers and men in the noble art of handling a vessel under sail.

For many years the *Viking* was painted white, but under the care of the navy she was restored to her original colours of black, gold and var-nishwork. Her appearance seems to have been enhanced by this decorative scheme of a bygone age. In 1948 she was sold out of the navy to the Todd family.

Throughout her life the *Viking* has carried a very striking figurehead of one of the old Viking sailors. It is a remarkably clever piece of work-manship, and sets off the bow of the yacht to perfection. It is believed this is the only yacht in

The famous *Viking* in a unique
photograph taken by Henry Win-
kelmann in 1897, only three years
after her launching. The original
rigging presents a fascinating sight.
The bowsprit and topmast are
housed and the mizzen has been
doused.

Viking racing in the early 1970s,
clearing out of Wellington Harbour
in a Cook Strait race.

New Zealand waters at the present time to carry a figurehead. It serves to remind us of the beautiful square-rigged ships of 100 years ago.

This veteran yacht, still sound in plank and possessing a picturesque old-world beauty en-tirely lost in a modern craft, is a notable example of the fine materials and sound workmanship incorporated in the yachts built by Charles Bailey Senior.

The grand old ship as she is today, *Viking* in later years, cruising in the Marlborough Sounds in 1968. Her original rigging long gone, she is now a Bermuda-rigged ketch and her cockpit is enclosed.

4.

The yachts of Charles Bailey Junior

AS WE HAVE SEEN, Charles Bailey Junior went into partnership with his brother Walter on the retirement of his father, the business becoming known as C. and W. Bailey Ltd. However, as is sometimes inevitable with family partnerships, the relationship did not work. Walter left his brother, and started in partnership with another boatbuilder called Bill Lowe. Their opposition company was called Bailey and Lowe Ltd., later to be known as W. S. Lowe and Son on Walter's death.

Undaunted, Charles continued building and designing yachts, launches and commercial craft. For the next 50 years many fine vessels slipped down his launching ways.

There is no doubt that the versatility of Bailey Junior stimulated much of the keen rivalry of the early days of Auckland yacht racing, for he would design almost any type of racing craft that was ordered from his firm. Commencing with the smaller classes, he gradually blossomed forth until at the height of his career he was building first-class racing yachts for New Zealand and Australia and practically monopolising the building of trading vessels for the islands. It is a great pity that it is not possible to reproduce some plans of his earliest boats, for with the passing of the years nearly all have gone astray.

From 1879, when he built his first boat, the 4.9 m *Elsie*, by candle-light, Charles went quickly ahead in the small classes. The names of such boats as *Gertie, Vic, Pat, Arrow, Gladys, Ira, Beata* and *Lad*, all centreboarders ranging from 4.8 to 6 m, may serve to stir the memories of some of the older generation of New Zealand yachtsmen.

Most of these boats must have been built at night after the day's work in the shipyard was over, for Charles, who originally supplied this list to Ronald Carter, put a bracket round the names, with the brief notation "by candle-light".

Next on his list we learn that he built the cutter *Minerva* for Mr J. Russell — 7.3 m on the waterline, with "cutwater and counter-stern". It was followed by the 9 m waterline *Rogue* for the same owner; this boat is still in service in Wellington, sailing under the name of *Muritai*. There was also the *Daisy*, built for a Mr W. Lind in 1893. This fine yacht was converted to a yawl rig in 1931, and was wrecked at Matakana in 1939. By this time conditions must have improved slightly, for Charles says these later boats were built under gaslight!

There is no greater proof of Charles Bailey's unbounded enthusiasm and innate love of yachtbuilding. He would forsake his leisure hours, working far into the night, so that he might fashion in wood the latest idea in his active brain.

In 1893 he commenced building a number of successful cutters in quick succession. Many yachtsmen know of such vessels as the *Rangatira*, which was built in 1894 for Mr W. Chatfield and met her end in 1921 when she fell from her cradle while being slipped; the *Atlanta*, which was built in 1894 for Messrs W. Canning and I. Smith (this cutter later raced with great success on Wellington Harbour); *Zinita; Constance*, which was wrecked in Auckland in the 1920s; *Cooee*, built in 1908 and still sailing in the Bay of Islands. There were the 7.32 m mullet boats, *Laura* and *Mizpah*. Another well known Bailey-built cutter was the *Heartsease*, for Mr A. B. Donald, a well-known Auckland merchant. *Heartsease* achieved some fame when she was sailed to Sydney in 1931 on the first leg of a world cruise. On reaching Sydney, the crew split up and the *Heartsease* was sold, never to return to Auckland.

The Bailey-designed gaff-rigged cutter *Speedwell*. She was wrecked on Waiheke Island in 1958.

But this is passing from 1893 to present-day yachts, for a number of these boats are still with us. It is necessary to retrace our steps and describe some of the earliest crack yachts built by Charles Junior — vessels whose names still conjure up memories of some of the keenest and most exciting racing in the early history of New Zealand yachting.

Shortly before 1900, Charles was commissioned by Mr A. T. Pittar of Auckland to build a 9 m linear-rater; the *Meteor*, as she was named, soon made intercolonial yachting history. Writing in the *New Zealand Illustrated Magazine* in April 1909 Frank Coombes says:

"Some three seasons ago, when the writer, who for many years was closely identified with the sport in Sydney, came to Auckland to reside, he was naturally much struck with the many fine yachts belonging to the port. At that time, and

for some two years previously, the crack yacht of her class in Port Jackson (Australia), was the *Bronzewing*, a two and a half rater built by the great Scottish designer Watson. This smart little racer's great deeds had virtually extinguished the class which she represented, as no other could approach her for speed. In Auckland, however, there was a yacht with a somewhat similar reputation, this being the 9.00 m *Meteor*. The writer immediately conceived the idea of an intercolonial match between these champions. Mr A. T. Pittar, the owner of the Aucklander and a very keen enthusiast, was immediately willing to cross the Tasman Sea, while the Royal Sydney Yacht Squadron at once accepted the challenge on behalf of the *Bronzewing*. Very great interest was taken in the encounter, but up to the last Sydney yachtsmen refused to believe in the possibility of defeat for their favourite, whose sail plan was altered and improvements made in every possible way.

"The result of the encounter came as a surprise to the water-loving folk on the other side, for in the races *Meteor* completely outsailed the *Bronzewing*, winning the match very easily.

"Another race of an intercolonial character occurred during the following season. This was a championship for one-raters, and took place on the Waitemata. The Auckland fleet were opposed by Mr Rymill's *Geisha*, of the Royal South Australian Yacht Squadron, and Mr S. Hordern's *Bronzewing IV* of the Sydney Amateur Sailing Club. Victory rested with the Aucklander *Laurel* (built and owned by Charles Bailey Junior) after a hard fight with *Bronzewing*, and the Logan boat *Mercia*."

The foregoing account of these two victories will serve to demonstrate the skill possessed by this clever young shipbuilder. To have beaten such a notable vessel as the *Bronzewing* was indeed a feather in his cap, and Charles was to receive further honours shortly after as the result of these two matches.

The champion Aucklander *Laurel* had meantime been purchased by a Sydney yachtsman, Mr J. Chinnery, who had an earnest desire to outsail Mr S. Hordern's new cutter *White Wings*, designed by the famous Will Fife of Scotland. During one of his visits to Australia, Bailey was asked by Chinnery if he thought he could build a boat to beat the Sydney champion. Charles paid a visit to the spot where *White Wings* was hauled out of the water. After he had carefully sized her up, he announced that he felt confident that he could build a boat to beat her. Thus it came about that the famous Auckland yacht *Bona* was built. She was sent over to Australia and eventually beat *White Wings*.

Another fast yacht built by Charles Junior about this time was the two and a half-rater *Thelma* for Mr S. S. Bannister. She was the champion in her class at Dunedin, racing on Port Chalmers harbour; on two occasions her owner took her north to Lyttelton, where she proved victorious.

Perhaps one of the most famous of the smaller cutters built by Bailey was the little *Speedwell*. She was built in 1907 to the order of Mr W. A. Wilkinson, who raced her for some years. She measured 9.7 m overall, 2.1 m in beam, and had a draught of 1.5 m. Throughout her life she carried the gaff cutter rig. For over 25 years this little flyer was owned by Messrs F. Cloke (who

The famous old trading cutter *Janet*, racing in the anniversary regatta in 1901.

The gaff rig to perfection. Bailey's *Waione* winning the Devonport Yacht Club's Duder Cup race in 1933.

Waione drifts past HMS *Chatham* on Auckland harbour in 1922.

died in 1976) and J. Patrick, who sailed her to victory on countless occasions. She was wrecked at Oneroa, Waiheke Island in 1961.

W. A. Wilkinson, for whom *Speedwell* was built, was a pioneer of Auckland yachting. A man small in stature, he had a fog horn of a voice, and after a career in yachting journalism founded the first yachting magazine in New Zealand — a weekly called *New Zealand Yachtsman* — in 1909. This magazine was published until 1939 when "Wilkie", as he was known to all, founded the Speedwell Yacht Agency, a brokerage company. At the time of his death in 1951 Wilkie owned the fine schooner *Queen Charlotte*.

There is another well-known yacht of the same length as the *Speedwell*, built two years before. This earlier cutter was christened the *Janet*, and under her Bermudian rig she is a familiar sight today on the Waitemata Harbour, racing on occasions in various yacht club fixtures. The *Janet* was built in Bailey's yard by his foreman, Angus Sutherland. Sutherland also

built the fast B-class cutter *Waione* (still afloat on Auckland harbour) in 1909 at the back of Holy Trinity Church, Devonport. Charles Bailey Junior designed *Waione* and closely supervised her construction. Angus Sutherland, who lived in Devonport, was the father of Morley Sutherland, who fathered ferro-cement construction of pleasure boats in New Zealand. Morley Sutherland died tragically young in 1972.

One of the largest pleasure yachts constructed by Bailey in the early days was the 60-tonne schooner-yacht *La Carabine*, built in 1903 to the order of an Australian sportsman. The following is an extract taken from the *New Zealand Herald* on 18 August 1903:

Sir Rupert Clark, the well-known Victorian sportsman, accompanied by his brother, Mr Ernest Clark, arrived from Sydney by the *Westralia* on Sunday night, and upon landing at the Queen Street Wharf on Monday morning was extended a cordial welcome on behalf of the local yachtsmen by Mr C. P. Murdoch, Commodore of the Royal New Zealand Yacht Squadron.

"During the forenoon, Sir Rupert paid a visit

The kind of yachting which makes the blood tingle. *Waione* reaching fast at around 10 knots under jib and staysail, a rig not seen very often today.

to the shipbuilding yards of Mr C. Bailey Junior, Custom Street West, in order to inspect the 60-tonne schooner-yacht *La Carabine* now being built to his order. In the course of an interview, Sir Rupert said: 'I am more than pleased with the appearance of the yacht, and the manner in which the work is being carried out. I had no idea, though, that you had such beautiful timber in New Zealand, and I know something about that material, too, for I have done a good deal of business with sawmillers in New South Wales. I have, however, never seen such beautiful timber as I saw in my visit to the shipyards today. When I had the designs of the yacht which I intended to build sent to me, they came from all parts of the world, and on my visit to Britain I had a good look around the shipyards, but saw nothing to equal the design as submitted by Mr Bailey, and I therefore accepted his contract. There was no favouritism in the matter at all, and I think it is a feather in Auckland's cap that she should compete with the outside world in the matter'."

La Carabine proved to be a fast vessel, and it is said that Sir Rupert remarked that she was one of the finest yachts he had ever set foot upon. Some years ago it was reported that *La Carabine* was still afloat, the property of a wealthy Chinese in New Guinea. Later Charles was to build another vessel for Sir Rupert, a 40-tonne ketch named the *Era*.

Seventy years ago Charles Bailey's yard was one of the busiest in the Southern Hemisphere. Besides fulfilling the many orders made on the firm for pleasure yachts, the yards were commissioned to construct a large number of vessels for the Pacific Island trade. The Tongan Government issued numerous orders for trading vessels, amongst them the cutters *Kologoou*, *Taufovu*, *Melino*, *Naitiae*, *Volokylie*, *Hifofua* and the *Koe-Fetuu-Aho* (for the Tongan Free Church).

He also built the schooners *Vitae* and *Tiare-Taporo* (the latter an auxiliary vessel 32 m long) for Messrs A. B. Donald for use in the Pacific trade. His name became a household word among people living in the Pacific.

His crowning achievement was the building of a very fine cutter yacht named the *Onelua* for the Tongan royal family. She measured 16 m overall, 3.3 m in beam, and drew 2 m of water. She was of three-skin, diagonal construction, and carried a big gaff cutter rig. This 11 m linear rater was considered to be Bailey's best effort amongst the big cutters, and on her maiden

passage to Tonga in 1917, under trysail and staysail, she sailed the distance of 1770 odd kilometres in the astonishing time of seven days. However this fine cutter had a very short life — a few years after her launching she went ashore on a reef in the South Pacific and became a total wreck.

After the *Onelua* the last yacht of any size to be built by Charles was the first-class cutter *Prize* for Mr W. Endean. She was constructed on the three-skin, diagonal principle, and measures 13 m overall, 9.7 m on the waterline by 3.3 m in the beam. She is a fast and handsome yacht, and has won many races since she was launched in 1921.

After the launching of the *Prize*, Charles constructed many fine power craft of various types and sizes, but the only other sailing craft of any note to be constructed by the firm were the forerunners of the present-day X-class restricted at 4.3 m. The first of these craft, the *Desert Gold*, was designed and constructed by Glad Bailey, under the ever-watchful eye of his father. In a later chapter will be found the story of how these boats came to be built and the position they held in New Zealand yachting.

At the age of 75 years Charles Junior supervised the building of his last yacht design. The vessel was launched towards the end of 1939 and was christened *The New Golden Hind*.

She was built to the order of Mr H. R. Jenkins of Kerikeri, who spent many years afloat cruising in the Hauraki Gulf. With a lifelong experience behind him, Charles had no difficulty in laying down the lines of the new vessel, which measures 28.6 m overall, 22.8 m on the waterline, 6.7 m in the beam, and 3.8 m draught of water — the displacement being 101 tonnes. The hull was built of kauri pine on the three-skin diagonal principle, and the deck trim was of teakwood. Her ballast, which is all inside, consisted of 25 tonnes of iron, cemented into her bilges. The vessel carried a lofty Bermudian ketch rig on her 30.5 m foremast, and a 21.3 m mizzen. She carried 130 sq m of canvas in her mainsail, 67 sq m in the mizzen, 40 sq m in the staysail, and 40 sq m in the jib, the total area in her working canvas being 278 sq m. She also carried a jib tops'l of 39 sq m and a squaresail yard on her foremast, which spread another 93 sq m of canvas.

Below decks *The New Golden Hind* was fitted out in what was described as "solid comfort". Besides the eight two-berth staterooms and the

The scow *Lena*, built by Bailey and Lowe in 1905. This was the smallest scow built and was used to carry waste material to the Riverhead paper mills, ferrying ceramic pipes from Hobsonville on the return journey.

One of the few photographs taken on board a scow. The crew are cleaning the deck. Note the fore-end of the centreboard case in the foreground.

Bailey's famous ketch *New Golden Hind*, his last yacht design and one of his finest. She was fitted out in what was described as "solid comfort".

four-berth forecastle, there was a noble saloon which measured 6 m long by 3.8 m wide. Athwart her mainmast on the port side was a large and finely-appointed galley with all the latest electrical appliances. Her main saloon and staterooms were panelled in a most artistic manner with New Zealand native woods, showing off without any ostentation one of the finest yacht interiors to be found in the Southern Hemisphere. In her well-appointed engineroom was installed a 66 h.p. Kelvin diesel engine.

The vessel was built at Opua in the Bay of Islands by Deeming Bros., who spent over two years working on her. At 10 a.m. on 7 July 1939 *The New Golden Hind* was launched with due ceremony from her builders' yard. With her big sticks lashed on deck, she steamed down to Auckland under her diesel engine power. In Auckland her masts were stepped, her rigging set up, and various small jobs above and below decks completed.

Shortly after her fitting out, her owner and party left for a cruise to the South Pacific, returning some time later full of praise for this beautiful sea-going vessel. She was a great tribute to her designer and builders, and at the time of her launching enjoyed the proud position of being New Zealand's largest and most powerful pleasure yacht. During World War II she was commandeered for service with the Royal New Zealand Air Force, and was later sold to the Pacific Islands.

Charles Bailey Junior passed away in 1949. With his death an era of New Zealand yachting came to an end. The influence that father and son had on the sport not only in New Zealand but also in Australia cannot be measured. New Zealand was indeed fortunate to have men of their genius; their impact is still to be felt in yacht design and construction today.

The *Mizpah*, built by Charles Bailey Junior in 1894 as a gaff cutter, clears the Okahu Bay boat harbour, re-rigged as gaff yawl, in 1952.

A fine study of a veteran keeler. *Atlanta*, built in Auckland in 1894 by Charles
Bailey Junior, sails on Wellington Harbour, where she has spent most of her life.

5.

The ill-fated *Strathcona*

CHARLES BAILEY JUNIOR produced many hundreds of fine vessels, but there was one alone which was his proudest creation. The master craftsman himself often asked people: "Did you see my schooner *Strathcona* before she was lost? She was a beauty."

Charles was right. She was a beauty, and if ever a man loved one of his own creations, he surely proved it in his unwavering affection for the *Strathcona*. It was said that when the news reached Auckland that the schooner had become a total wreck, Charles was for many a long day a very saddened man.

In 1915 the Pacific Cable Board called for tenders for the building of a schooner to be used for carrying employees and stores from Honolulu to the remote cable station situated on Fanning Island, one of the loneliest coral atolls in the northern Pacific.

Charles Bailey Junior's tender for £10,000 was accepted, and the keel of the fastest schooner ever to have sailed out of the Hauraki Gulf was laid down. Drawing on the vast store of knowledge he now possessed, after nearly a lifetime of experience, Charles laid out the lines of the *Strathcona*. She was built of picked heart-of-kauri pine planking, fastened to sawn pohutukawa frames, and she measured 33.5 m overall, 7.3 m on the beam, and 3.6 m draught of water.

When her moulds went up, yachtsmen and seafaring men in Auckland came and inspected the latest effort of Bailey Junior. Critical eyes ran past her fine entrance and moved slowly up the clean sweeping lines of her run. When she was fully planked up there were many exclamations of surprise and delight from those who had watched her building. Here, without a doubt, was Bailey's masterpiece.

Said one old salt to the builder one day: "You know, Charles, this little schooner of yours will be the fastest vessel that will ever go out of Auckland under sail." He was probably right,

for no other sail trading vessel at that time equalled her for speed.

Piece by piece the many thousands of component parts went carefully into the perfect ship, and around the month of May she stood ready for the launch. Yet Dame Fortune must have been smiling quietly to herself as she watched all this loving care and attention being bestowed on this beautiful piece of fabric: the little ship was eventually doomed to a very short life. But nobody knew it in May 1915. They launched her with due ceremony, and as she started on the ways on her short run to the water, the splinters of glass from the champagne bottle shone in the bright sunshine as the wine ran stickily down her white cut-water.

When she was rigged and ready for her trials, a distinguished gathering of seamen collected on her poop deck. In a light nor'east breeze she slowly worked her way out into the Rangitoto Channel. Representing the owners were Captain Holmes, of the cable ship *Iris*, and the chief engineer, William Foster. Charles Bailey himself was also there, and many others. They hauled her on the wind, they ran her free, and then Charles, who had the wheel, suggested that they wear her (that is, change direction).

"Stand by to wear ship!" he called.

The *Strathcona* swung round on her keel, almost in her own length. She was so perfectly balanced that a boy could steer her on a wind, so light was she on her helm.

The patent log of the *Iris* was on board. It was tested and guaranteed correct. They streamed it from the taffrail, and for half an hour the *Strathcona's* speed was recorded by stopwatch; she was logging eight and a half knots in a light breeze. On a broad lead she was later reputed to have reached a speed of 15 knots. She was a beauty to look at, as well as being a witch for speed.

Shortly after, on a Friday afternoon, she sailed on her maiden voyage with 13 souls on board. Captain Holmes, Charles Bailey and a number of other folk who had come to bid her farewell, dropped over the *Strathcona's* rail into the builder's waiting launch as the ship was outward bound on her voyage to Fanning Island. On that fateful Friday afternoon they saw her head for the open sea with her 13 men. Hull down was the last her builder ever saw of her.

As she disappeared down channel, Captain Holmes turned to Charles. "Well Bailey," he said, "she is a mighty fine little ship; you must be very proud of her. I wonder what her fortune is to be?" He little knew that her life was nearly over.

Sailing on a north-easterly course, the *Strathcona* was daily getting nearer her burial ground. Only six days out she was to tear her bottom out and break her back in the most notorious spot in the South Pacific, the North Minerva Reef. But let us go back to that midwinter afternoon 62 years ago and endeavour to trace the movements of the schooner on the only ocean passage she ever made.

It was on a Friday afternoon early in the month of June 1915 when she headed out to sea on her maiden voyage. She was running with a light breeze under all plain sail and her auxiliary engine. Towards midnight the wind had breezed up until the ship was tearing along at a speed of over 12 knots, and orders were given to shut off the engine. Shortly after, she had the Cuvier Light abeam and took her departure from this point.

Throughout Saturday the wind continued to blow freshly from the sou'west, the fores'l and mainsail being double-reefed in the forenoon watch. Because the gear was all brand new and stretching, the watch on deck were constantly sweating up on the halyards. However the ship was behaving splendidly and driving along in fine style. The wind remaining fair, hopes were entertained for a fast passage.

The third and fourth days passed uneventfully, and on the fifth the wind moderated, allowing the crew to shake out the double-reefed fore and mainsail. The wind throughout the passage had remained in the same quarter, blowing from light to strong from the south-west. On the afternoon of the sixth and last day the ship was bowling along at a 10 to 11-knot clip.

It was midwinter. The tropical sun sinking quickly caused darkness to settle down on the water before 6 p.m. The watch on deck had been ordered to keep a sharp lookout for reefs ahead, and just before the last of the daylight was blotted out, Lilburn, the second mate, searched the horizon through a telescope but saw nothing but sea and sky. At one bell, 7.45 p.m., the *Strathcona* was sailing at 11 knots with the wind on her starboard quarter when suddenly a great cry came from the lookout man:

"Breakers ahead under the lee bow. Hard up on your helm!"

The second mate, hearing the cry, leaped for the foresail sheet, and having flattened it in was running aft to assist on the main when *Strathcona* struck. In vain the man on the wheel tried to get the ship up into the wind but owing to her great speed and the breakers into which she was plunging she would not answer her helm. She struck the North Minerva Reef with gigantic force at the top of high water.

The second mate, who jumped for the main rigging when she struck, saw her bow rise high into the air while a terrible tearing sound came from underneath as her keel ploughed through the coral. She came to rest half out of the water, her sails still drawing steadily. Less than a month from her launching this beautiful piece of fabric had sailed her first and last passage.

A quick survey of the position revealed that the *Strathcona's* keel was broken in two and ripped right out of the ship aft of amidships. The tremendous downward thrust of the after portion of the hull, which was hanging over deep water, had broken the rudder stock off just below the trunk, and the blade, springing upwards with the broken section of the keel, had pierced the hull between two frames. The engineroom down aft was quickly flooded and half of the keel was floating alongside the hull. Sadly the men realised that the little ship was done for.

The North Minerva Reef, which is a small coral atoll in the making, had been awash when the ship struck, but next day at low water the crew were able to put the launch and whaleboat overboard and haul them out upon the exposed coral reef. Here the boats were provisioned, and as the tide rose they were floated across and anchored in the lagoon. There were eight men, including the captain and second mate in the 6.7 m launch, and four men in the charge of the first mate in the 4.9 m whaleboat.

Their position was far from enviable. The first year of the Great War was drawing to a close, and shipping, like everything else was disorganised. The men could hold out faint hope of being picked up by a passing vessel. Much of the water had been lost when the ship struck; the tank connections had been broken, emptying the precious fluid into the flooded bilges. Added to this was the problem of conserving their food supply for an indefinite period, as they knew some considerable time must elapse before the vessel was posted as missing and a search begun for them. But perhaps their greatest danger was from the elements. Had a very severe storm broken over the low lying reef there seemed every possibility that their boats would be overwhelmed or swept out to sea.

The men suffered great discomfort in the two small boats, especially at night when they were trying to rest. Finally they decided to construct a raft and live on board.

The *Strathcona's* masts and spars were cut away, and under the supervision of the second mate a big raft was built, anchored on top of the reef by wire hawsers. In a rude shelter of awnings, the men bunked down at night on narrow wooden platforms constructed high enough off the raft to prevent the sea reaching them. In bad weather, which several times visited the reef, they were constantly up to their waists in flying water. At the going out and coming in of the tide, the raft was severely buffeted about, adding greatly to their discomfort.

Under these miserable conditions the men lived precariously, until on the 16th day, with no sign of help forthcoming, the captain made a momentous decision to put to sea in the launch and seek help from the nearest inhabited island, Ono-I-Lau, some 300-odd kilometres away. He took with him the mate, the cook and two able seamen, one of whom had charge of the engine. The rest of the ship's company was left behind in the care of the second mate, who had orders to stand by until rescued. As a last resort he was to put to sea in the whaleboat.

With the departure of the captain's boat, misfortune overcame the castaways. Water supplies began to run short, and for nine days they knew the agonies of thirst. They also suffered a great deal from bad cuts caused by sharp coral.

But Lilburn rose to the occasion and made preparations for securing a supply of water when the rains came. He ran a connecting pipe from the top of the flat main deckhouse of the wrecked schooner through a hole in the deck, and into a spare 2275 l tank which was lying in the hold undamaged. One evening heavy rainclouds were seen approaching and soon the first comforting raindrops were hitting the men's

upturned faces. Stripping off their clothes, they stood in the pelting rainstorm, while down below in the *Strathcona's* engineroom the tank was soon filled to overflowing. To save the labour of carrying the water to the raft, a number of galvanised iron pipes, taken from amongst the cargo, were connected to a pump on the tank and led down to the raft.

But the life of the men was getting daily more unbearable. The strain of waiting for rescue was beginning to tell on their constitutions. Then one day, while the second mate was sitting in the shelter writing up his diary (which he never failed to keep) he asked one of the men to take the telescope and see if he could see any signs of a ship. Only a short time had elapsed when the man came back greatly excited, saying he thought he saw smoke on the horizon. Shortly after, a ship was seen coming up fast to the reef. Their troubles were over at last, and next morning His Majesty's cable ship *Iris* sent a boat through the passage into the lagoon to greet the mate, who was sailing out to meet it in the whaleboat. After spending 25 miserable anxious days on the reef the castaways were taken off and the *Iris* stood out to sea.

In the meantime, the captain's boat had reached Ono safely. After some delay the skipper had managed to charter a small native cutter. They were actually not far from the reef on the return journey when they were sighted by the *Iris*. The rest of the *Strathcona's* company were taken on board.

Uninsured, the schooner was a total loss. She was finally sold to the late Captain Ross of Auckland, who said he would go down and attempt to salvage her. But one look at the vessel convinced him that she was beyond all hope of repair. After stripping her of all useful gear he in turn presented the remains to Captain Crawford, who likewise realised that she was useless. There on the reef, it is said, are lying the remains to this day. They left her there, a pitiful, broken derelict, a sight to sadden the heart of any real sailorman. She certainly deserved a better fate, for she had none of the vices common amongst some ships.

She killed no man at her launching; she did not even hang on the ways, which is always regarded as an omen of ill-luck. No man fell from aloft, or lost his life off her big, raking jib-boom. She was a clean ship; she was a beauty to look at; she sailed fast, and steered with the ease of a racing yacht.

And yet, one wonders if all was really well! Old sailors from the great Cape Horn windships have handed down some strange superstitions through the years. For example, they say it is courting disaster to commence a voyage on a Friday. Was the *Strathcona* doubly condemmed when she sailed on this day with 13 souls on board?

The story of the *Strathcona* is one of the strange and little-known dramas of the South Pacific. Out there on the North Minerva Reef she fell apart as the great storms surged through and over her once-stout timbers. Only the birds of the sea, wheeling to pause in their flight, witnessed the end of the story.

An open mullet boat setting sail for the Auckland fishing grounds in 1903.

6.

The mullet boat

IN COUNTLESS SEAPORT towns throughout the world will be found many different types of local craft engaged in coastwise trading and deep sea or offshore fishing. Two distinct types, the scows and the mullet boats, are to be found in Auckland today; the former are slowly disappearing, but the mullet boats are increasing in numbers each year.

These latter vessels are "local" in every sense of the word, for they belong to no other port, either in New Zealand or throughout the world. The name "mullet boat" dates back to the very early days of New Zealand's colonisation, and although there is no record of the first boat built in Auckland, there is sufficient evidence to enable us to say that the type was evolved somewhere around 1880.

The boats were designed for a specific purpose — the netting of mullet, which abound in the shallow tidal reaches, creeks and estuaries of the Hauraki Gulf and its environs. Fishermen wanted in the first instance a shoal-draught boat. Next they required a craft that could beat up against the tidal river currents under sail. Lastly, they needed for economy's sake a boat which could be handled by a small crew. So in the early types which were the predecessors of the present day craft was found the ideal combination.

The early boats measured some 8-8.5 m overall. They had a beam of 2.4-2.7 m and drew about 600 mm of water with the centreboard drawn up. With the board lowered, the total draught reached some 1.8-2.1 m. There is no verification of the exact measurements of the very earliest boats, but the above details are not far enough out to be of any great consequence.

The earliest boats were built with single-skin kauri pine planking on sawn pohutukawa frames, but later the sawn frames were discarded and the present-day method of using steambent timbers was introduced. The boats had a short fore and aft deck and narrow side decks, the main portion of the boats being open. Raised coamings ran round inside the decking, so turning off any water which was coming aboard.

The vessels were designed with a plumb stem and upright tuck stern, the latter being broad and shallow. The keel, which carried a wide keelson, was well rockered throughout its length, and the midship section showed a broad bottom without any hollow in the garboards, good deadrise terminating in a fairly hard bilge at the waterline. The centreboard trunk was built up with solid timber bolted right through the keel, and housed a heavy iron rectangular plate swinging from a kingbolt and controlled by a chain or wire rope running over a sheave on the after end of the centreboard trunk. The type of centreboard which has the projecting arm on the forward end was introduced in later craft, and is more or less universal amongst these boats today.

The mullet boats carried a moderate cutter rig on a pole mast and bowsprit projecting about 2.5 m outboard. They were steered by a big "barndoor' rudder hung on pintles on the tuck stern. The bowsprit heel rested in the bitts, and was held down by the usual type of gammon band, either to one side of a projecting stem head, or over the top if the stem was cut off at deck level. A heavy iron or gunmetal rod or chain bobstay pulled the bowsprit down in a fine sweeping curve, counter-balancing the upward thrust of the sheer in the foredeck. Bowsprit shrouds leading aft to guyplates set well back on the sheerplanks were bowsed taut by means of tarred lanyards.

A ring traveller and outhaul was hooked to the jib tack, allowing the sail to be set flying at any point along the bowsprit, thereby balancing the mainsail when it was reefed down. The staysail tack was shackled at the stem head, and the sail hanked to the forestay, both headsails being hoisted by means of a block purchase tackle.

The mainsail was laced to the boom and gaff,

and had mast hoops on the luff, while a bridle and traveller on the boom and gaff carried the blocks of the mainsheet and peak halyards.

The heel of the mainboom had hardwood pohutukawa jaws which rested on top of a wooden saddle; this provided a rest for the sail and spars when they were stowed. The curved hardwood jaws of the gaff were provided with a concave wooden "tumbler", which allowed the gaff to slide easily up and down the mast. At the top of the tumbler, a small sheave was let in, taking the place of a pulley block, for the throat halyard purchase. Both the boom and gaff jaws were held to the mast by means of a parrel consisting of small hardwood balls, threaded on a piece of light line, which passed through holes bored in the ends of the jaws.

Underneath the flooring inside, about 1500 kg of lead or pig iron ballast was stowed well along the keel and out on the bilges amidship. The manner in which the ballast was stowed had a great deal to do with the sailing qualities of the mullet boats. Today the distribution of these weights has become a fine art amongst mullet boat skippers.

In practice, the mullet boats ably lived up to all that was expected of the design. They were fast on or off a wind, sailing with a slow, easy motion in a seaway, and pointing well on the wind; but it was when running or reaching that they really showed their paces, for with a hard breeze on the quarter, these boats could log from eight to nine knots without undue effort.

With a crew of one or two men, the early mullet boats would set out for the fishing grounds. When the sails were lowered and stowed, one of the crew would man a long pair of sweeps. Pulling steadily on the oars, he would send the mullet boat forward in a big arc, while down aft the net which had already been neatly coiled down would pay out steadily over the broad tuck stern. In due course the net ends would be steadily closed in again, and as the net came back over the tuck, the fish would be extracted and tossed into the fish well.

When night came on, the crew would anchor in a sheltered spot. Placing a narrow hatch-covering over the forward portion of the coamings, they would bunk down under this and the foredeck. Their cooking was often done over an open oil drum punched with holes; it would have a layer of sand on the bottom to prevent the heat penetrating to the floorboards. These oil drum braziers, though crude in appearance, were most efficient in practice, providing ample heat both for cooking and for warming the cabin on cold nights.

And so the mullet boat fishermen pursued their simple calling. With a full load of fish aboard they would hasten home to the fish wharves, where their catch would be sold. Much of the mullet so caught was destined for canning. On the Kaipara Harbour an industry of this kind was carried on for some years. As soon as the last of the fish was out, the mullet boats would be thoroughly cleaned and the gear and nets overhauled, ready to set out for the grounds again.

Fishing from these open boats in bad weather was a hard life, but it was not unpleasant — many good yarns are told of the lives of the mullet boat fishermen. Today they have all gone. Not one mullet boat is engaged in fishing, and it would be a difficult task to search out half a dozen mullet boats that had ever been engaged in the calling for which they were designed.

The fishing mullet boats have been displaced by modern diesel-engined craft measuring anything up to 18 m and possessing comfortable crew's quarters which compare favourably with any to be found in a well-kept pleasure vessel. No longer do fishermen have to slog up the harbour in the teeth of a westerly gale in a heavily-laden mullet boat; today they steer their high-wooded, powerful fishing vessels from the warmth and comfort of a glassed-in wheelhouse.

It may be asked why so much has been said about a fishing vessel when our subject is yachting. The fact of the matter is that quite early in the history of these craft, yachtsmen realised their possibilities. It was not long before the mullet boats were being used for cruising and racing. Today they form a large percentage of Auckland's yachting fleet, and with their numbers steadily increasing it would appear that the craft will always be popular.

In the early days of the mullet boats there was a strange combination of circumstances which induced a yachtsman to look amongst the fishing fleet when requiring a mullet boat for pleasure purposes. When they were eventually nearly all taken over for this purpose, one might even have found an occasional fisherman looking amongst the pleasure boats when requiring a craft to go fishing! Some of Auckland's one-time fishing vessels proved champions, the 7.92 m mullet boat *Omatere*, built by the Logan brothers, being a notable example.

One of the first mullet boats to be used for

A mullet boat on the slip for cleaning. Note the traveller on the bowsprit. In the foreground pohutukawa knees season before being used. Bailey and Lowes's yard, 1902.

pleasure purposes was the *Swallow*, owned by Mr J. Lomey, who in 1886 won the Auckland Anniversary Regatta for fishing boats in a hard sou'westerly breeze. Old-timers such as *Manola*, *Welcome Jack* and *Venice* were built on the solid frame principle. Some are still in commission, although most of them have been converted into auxiliaries.

The *Manola*, which was rather deep-hulled for fishing, was purchased by a Mr Holderness in 1886 and used as a pleasure craft. In the following years such boats as the *Annie* and the *Flora* were built by the late Mr "Dadda" Reid. The *Rosie*, which was set up in frame by a Mr Drummond, was bought by Mr J. Clare, who finished building her. She ended her days destroyed by fire while lying in Islington Bay.

Another prominent boat was the *Shamrock*, owned by Mr H. McCormick, who sold her to a Mr Ryan. She was eventually lost with all hands. After selling the *Shamrock*, Mr Ryan decided to have a new boat built, and in 1902 commenced the building of a much more advanced type of mullet boat, one which was really the forerunner of the present-day craft. Clare and Collings, Auckland boatbuilders, were approached, and after drawing up the lines of two boats and setting them up in frame, they offered Mr McCor-

mick the choice of either yacht. He decided upon the well-known *Emerald*, while Clare and Collings kept the other craft, which was christened *Okere*. These two boats were at least 10 years ahead of the times, and easily defeated any of the existing yachts at that time.

Following the appearance of the *Emerald* and *Okere*, Mr R. Murphy ordered one of 6.7 m from Clare and Collings; so it came about that the famous old-time champion *Mowai* was built. At that time the late Mr J. Mackay, who formerly owned the *Echo* (7.3 m), placed an order with the same builders, resulting in the *Glady* being constructed. This craft had a great turn of speed, and flew the champion flag right up until the death of her owner.

Shortly after the advent of the *Glady*, Arch Logan designed and built the champions *Venus* (6.7 m), *Ngaire*, *Celox* and *Omatere* (all 7.9 m). All of these boats have been consistent prize-winners for many years. About the same time Collings and Clare built the champion *Ronaki* (7.9 m).

As these later boats were highly successful, and an entirely wholesome type, their measure-

A 7.9m (26 ft) mullet boat reaching down the harbour. A superb action shot from several decades ago.

ments were adopted by the various yacht clubs of the times. Succeeding craft were built to conform with the specifications. This was a wise move on the part of the officials, for mullet boat racing had begun to cause extreme rivalry among the various owners. With the passing of the years since they were first adopted for pleasure purposes, various changes had occurred. Chief amongst these alterations were an increase in beam and greatly enlarged sail plans.

To prevent the class from developing into an unwholesome racing machine, certain rules and conditions were now laid down. The dimensions for boats of 7.9 m (26 ft) then read: not more than 7.9 m overall, not less than 915 mm moulded depth and no more than 2.7 m in beam. The 7.3 m (24 ft) class dimensions read: not more than 7.3 m overall, not less than 915 mm moulded depth and not more than 2.6 m in beam. The 6.7 m (22 ft) class dimensions read: not more than 6.7 m overall, not less than 840 mm moulded depth and not more than 2.3 m in beam.

These dimensions remained in force for a number of years until they were finally revised to allow bigger boats to be built. The alterations in all three classes were as follows: for every 305 mm (12 in) of beam in excess of the existing measurements, 152 mm (6 in) to be added to the moulded depth. These measurements still hold good today, with the exception of the 6.7 m class. Because of the increasing popularity of this class (and the great rivalry amongst the various skippers to win the coveted Lipton Cup contest held each year) it was decided to allow a further change. This resulted in the following rule being laid down: the moulded depth in the 6.7 m (22 ft) class shall be one-third of the beam. This latest change in the measurement rule has resulted in a very wholesome and fast type of yacht. The only mullet boats racing today are to be found in the 6.7 m class.

Perhaps one of the best examples of this class today is the *Tamariki*, built in 1934. Many years had passed by since Mr C. J. Collings, who was formerly in partnership with Mr C. Clare, had built a mullet boat. But when he decided to challenge for the Lipton Cup he undoubtedly produced a champion in *Tamariki*. Not only did she win the cup as the representative of the Royal New Zealand Yacht Squadron, but she also won the Savory Cup at the Auckland Anniversary Regatta, the Anzac Points Cup and numerous first prizes in various yacht club fixtures.

Another notable craft built by Collings was the 7.9 m mullet boat *Corona* in 1936. This fine vessel had a beam of 3.2 m and spread no less than 83 sq m of sail in her working mainsail, jib and staysail. She carried a lofty gaff rig on her 12.2 m mast, with a 9 m mainboom, 5.8 m gaff and 4.5 m bowsprit. From bowsprit tip to end of mainboom, she measured 13.8 m which is the limit allowable for this class. Under her floor she carried 2.5 tonnes of ballast permanently stowed.

From these figures a general idea may be gained of the changes which have come about since one of the forerunners of this present-day class, the *Manola*, was built. Yachtsmen cannot fail to appreciate the enormous sail-carrying capacity of this yacht, which is slightly under 8 m, on the waterline. One pauses to consider how it is possible to sail this apparently grossly over-canvassed craft to advantage. Yet the 7.9 m class mullet boats sail remarkably well both on and off the wind, and have proved times without number that properly handled with a trained crew they are well able to stand up to hard driving in rough weather. The *Corona* once sailed from Little Barrier Island in the Hauraki Gulf to Leigh Harbour on the mainland, a distance of 22 km in one and a half hours, at an average speed of nine and a half knots, under whole mainsail in really heavy weather.

But it would be incorrect to say that the mullet boat has not got some disadvantages; most yachts have, for there is no such thing as a perfect ship. Perhaps the greatest drawback to the yachts, especially those of 7.9 m, is that they require a large crew. In heavy weather six men is not too many when racing or cruising off shore. Because of the large sail plans, the boats are hard to handle in a breeze, and the gear is subjected to great wear and tear if a vessel is constantly racing. This necessitates frequent replacements. On a wind under full sail it is not uncommon practice to put two men on the long tillers, and even then the ship sometimes takes charge in the hard puffs and gets her head up into the eye of the wind. On rare occasions mullet boats have been known to take the bit between their teeth and just clear out like a bolting horse until strong arms finally get them under control again. Another drawback is that the boats lack headroom; you will be lucky if you can get 1.2 m clear under the cabintop beams.

Apart from these small drawbacks, however, the boats are an ideal combination of speed and seaworthiness. They make a beautiful and impressive sight as they cross the starting line in a race under great masses of billowing white canvas. They carry enormous masthead spinnakers and leading jibs — and when these kites are set there is anything up to 112 sq m of canvas pulling the big ones along.

Fortunately, accidents are rare occurrences. The only serious mishap in the last 40-odd years occurred on board the big *Celox*. At the time she was running in company with a number of other yachts in a race to Matiatia. Shortly after passing through the **Motuihe Passage**, a fierce squall overtook the fleet. The *Celox* suddenly put her foredeck under water and went straight to the bottom, taking one of the crew and a young lad with her before the horrified yachtsmen on surrounding craft realised what was happening. The yacht was later raised to the surface.

Amongst some of the well-known 26-footers (7.9 m) may be mentioned the *Sadie, Waitere II, Bluestreak, Awatere, Spray* and what is often described as the sister ship of the *Celox*, the auxiliary yacht *Mona*, designed and built by the Logan brothers. Two others — the old *Calypso* and the more modern *Starloch*, built by Bayley and Tyre on the North Shore in 1914 – are both fine examples of shapely and fast yachts. The former craft was converted into a deadwood keel boat during the winter of 1939 after having her centreboard trunk removed. In the easterly gale which blew throughout Sunday, 10 December, 1939 *Calypso* broke her chain. Driving ashore, she smashed herself to matchwood in spite of the valiant efforts of yachtsmen and bystanders who did their best to save the old ship.

In the 6.7 m class may be found the names of many yachts, both old and modern, which will revive the memories of past and present mullet boat skippers and recall to mind many a hard-fought race. Prominent amongst the earlier boats was the sweetly-lined, red hulled *Venus*, the *Lucille*, *Valeria*, *Mowai*, and *Welcome Jack*; among later yachts were Dick Lang's *Forest Gold* (that was converted to a dead-wood keel boat), Lidgard Brothers' crack *Marie*, *Doreen*, *Waima* and *Rakoa*, (designed by Arch Logan and built by the late Joe Slattery). They were all good boats with splendid records, and many of them are still winning races today.

From the year 1880 to the present day is a long time, and it is interesting to note the growth and the changes which have come about during this period of nearly a century. As we have seen, the mullet boat has altered a great deal since the time the *Manola*, one of the first boats to be used for pleasure purposes, was built. As previously mentioned, she was somewhat narrow and deep-hulled, and her sail plan was on a moderate scale compared with that on vessels of her size today.

Yachtsmen and boatbuilders set about improving the boats to suit racing and cruising conditions. They still retained the general shape, but they increased the beam and also enlarged the measurement across the tuck. To produce a hull which could stand up more ably under the increased sail areas they added more ballast. Although the solid frames were substituted for steam-bent timbers, the boats did not suffer from structural weaknesses in any way.

Some of the older mullet boats were built of two skins, and still others were constructed on the deadwood principle. A later idea was to discard the cabintop set on coamings and build the boat with what is known as a "raised deck". These two latter features were incorporated in the 7.9 m mullet boat *Vigilant*, designed and built by Cox and Philmer, and launched from J.

Slattery's yard in 1934. This yacht carries a lofty Bermudian rig on her 15.25 m stick and is the first mullet boat to be equipped with wheel steering. But these alterations to the original type of mullet boat are the exception rather than the rule, and the *Vigilant* is the only boat of her type in Auckland today.

There have been few changes in crew accommodation. Of course quite early in their adoption as pleasure craft, the open portion of the boats was covered up by raising the coamings and laying a cabintop over cambered beams. On some of the smaller craft this cabintop is in two portions, the forward half being permanently fastened down, while the after portion is made to lift off when more room is required in the cockpit for racing or day sailing.

The interior of the majority of the mullet boats is invariably left wholly open, there being no bulkheads (with the exception of that which divides the cockpit from the cabin). Long bunks of good width run round the skin of the hull, providing sleeping room for four to six men, depending on the size of the yacht. The usual locker space is found round the square cockpit under the side and after decks. In these lockers are kept spare ropes and gear of all description, also water tanks, cooking appliances and food for use when cruising.

The greatest and most controversial change to mullet boats in 100 years was the decision in 1974 by the sponsoring club, the Ponsonby Cruising Club, to allow moulded fibreglass boats to be registered as L-class mullet boats and race against existing wooden yachts. There were dire predictions that the class would become dominated by glass boats. Some feared a subsequent loss of interest leading to the extinction of this famous type of boat, somewhat similar to what happened in the 4.3 m Jellicoe X-class. The club was well aware of this possibility, and proposed stringent specifications for this new method of construction. It was decided that the mould for the fibreglass construction should be taken off the well-known and well performed mullet boat *Taotane*, designed and built by Collings and Bell in 1935.

The first fibreglass 6.7 m mullet boat was launched in 1973. The innovation has actually boosted the class, in fact. Several top keeler skippers such as Jim Davern have been attracted to the class because of the close single design racing it offered.

Still, old-time mullet boat skippers and crews

would not recognise this new breed of yacht. It retains the mullet boat character, but it is a far cry from the old fishing boat pedigree. Gone is the old-fashioned, inefficient gaff rig with multiple headsails, set on wooden pole masts. Gone also are the cotton sails, double purchase headsail sheets and halyards. The barndoor rudder is retained, as are minimum restrictions on the amount of ballast carried, the length of the spinnaker pole (6.7 m, the length of the boat) and the spinnaker (it must not exceed 74.3 sq m). The gaff rig is replaced by a modern high-aspect ratio mainsail of terylene set on alloy spars, with a single overlap headsail, all handled with winches. The yachts remain great sail carriers, requiring agile and fit crews, to drive the powerful hulls.

The mullet boats race each year for the coveted Lipton Cup, presented for annual competition by Sir Thomas Lipton, of Americas Cup fame, in the 1920 and 1930 period. This beautiful trophy, valued at $1800, was presented in 1922 and is the oldest trophy still raced for by the same class in New Zealand yachting. Winners of the Lipton Cup since 1922 have been as follows:

1922 *Valeria*	1933 *Valeria*
1923 *Marie*	1934 *Komuri*
1924 *Marie*	1935 *Tamariki*
1925 *Marie*	1936 *Valeria*
1926 *Rakoa*	1937 *Tamariki*
1927 *Lucille*	1938 *Tamariki*
1928 *Valeria* and	1939 *Tamariki*
Varuna	1940 *Taotane*
1929 *Valeria*	1941 *Otira*
1930 *Marie*	1942 *Varmarie*
1931 *Marie*	1943 *Kohara*
1932 *Valeria*	1944 *Komuri*

1945 *Komuri*	1961 *Eranie*
1946 *Komuri*	1962 *Eranie*
1947 *Komuri*	1963 *Eranie*
1948 *Tamariki*	1964 *Controversy*
1949 *Varmarie*	1965 *Eranie*
1950 *Tamariki*	1966 *Taotane*
1951 *Tamariki*	1967 *Eranie*
1952 *Tamariki*	1968 *Tamariki*
1953 *Taotane*	1969 *Tiroa*
1954 *Taotane*	1970 *Taotane*
1955 *Taotane*	1971 *Karros*
1956 *Tamariki*	1972 *Karros*
1957 *Taotane*	1973 *Macushla*
1958 *Tamariki*	1974 *Tao Too*
1959 *Tamariki*	1975 *Honey*
1960 *Tamariki*	1976 *Orion*

There have been some hard names levelled at these yachts on many occasions — "workhouses, poor men's keel yachts" and so on. The life aboard has been likened to "spending a weekend under the dining room table" because of the lack of headroom. All this may be true, but never yet has anyone had the temerity to say: "Mullet boats cannot sail; they are not weatherly". Which, when one comes to consider these points from all angles, are the main virtues of any boat.

From time to time it is suggested that the name of "mullet boat" be altered to something more high-sounding. That anyone should wish to hide the identity of these popular racing yachts seems inappropriate. It is far more fitting that the name should be retained for all time, thereby perpetuating the memories of the humble fishermen who were directly responsible for introducing this splendid type of craft nearly 100 years ago.

7.

The Collings family

IN THE PREVIOUS CHAPTER we discussed Mr C. J. Collings and his influence on the development of the mullet boat. In fact the design influence and boatbuilding skill of Charles James Collings and Alexander John Collings, father and son, extended beyond mullet boats.

Charles Collings, the father, was born in Wellington in 1870 and was for several years apprenticed to the Auckland civil engineer Charles Edward Cooke. This apprenticeship was followed by a long period of employment with the most famous of all the old-time yacht designers and builders — Robert Logan Senior. The genius of this master craftsmen must have had a marked effect on the young journeyman.

In 1896 Collings married Anne Christine Nicholson, and left the employ of Logan, moving to Waitekauri (following the Waihi gold rush). Here he was engaged in contracting, building and designing houses, bridges and roads, as well as taking an active part in district activities such as the local volunteer fire brigade. His son Alex was born at Waitekauri in 1898, and in 1901 the family moved back to Auckland, where Charles established a boatbuilding yard, drawing on his experience with Robert Logan. The business thrived, and in 1902 he was joined in partnership by Mr W. Clare. Thus the company called Collings and Clare, which was to build so many fine pleasure craft, was established.

Alex Collings did not show much interest in boatbuilding initially, and left school to study accountancy. After several jobs in this field, none of which suited him, he turned, in 1918 to his true vocation — boatbuilding and designing. He joined his father's company, now called Collings and Bell, which was located on the St. Mary's Bay foreshore, adjacent to the old site of the Ponsonby Cruising Club. This famous boating area was completely built over with the development of the motorway to the Auckland Harbour Bridge in 1959. Commuters using this road do not realise what boating history they are driving over.

Alex Collings had a very shy nature, which as is so often the case was camouflaged by a gruff exterior. But his shyness was coupled with a brilliant academic mind, which resulted in the design and construction of many fast power boats as well as yachts. Indeed the first tank-testing of designs in New Zealand was conducted by Charles and Alex Collings in 1921.

Charlie Collings had some academic and practical training, plus a natural flair for the design and building of all types of small vessels. It was supplemented by a real enthusiasm for the sport, including racing.

It appears that Alex's academic mind started to influence the design of his father's boats in the early 1920s. Yet even after Charles Collings's death in 1946, the work still reflected the thinking of both men.

Charlie Collings was particularly well-known for his mullet boats, the first of which were the *Emerald* in 1902 and *Okere* and *Mowai* about the same period, all of which were champion 22-footers (6.7 m). *Ronaki* and *Corona* were 26-footers (7.9 m). *Corona*, built for Ron and Gordon Nunns, was the outstanding boat of her class. *Tamariki*, built in 1934, was a consistent winner of the Lipton Cup which she won 12 times, a record. She is undoubtedly New Zealand's most famous 6.7 m mullety.

They built fewer keelers, but all were sound ships. In 1936 they designed and built *Minerva* for Bunty Palmer, followed by *Cyrena* for Boy Bellve.

Ngatiawa and *Anthea II* were built after 1946. *Anthea II* was designed by McGruer of Scotland, who inspected her prior to launching while on his way to judge the 1956 Olympic Games yacht races in Australia. He complimented the yard on the workmanship. *Anthea II* was built for John Ellis, and *Ngatiawa* was designed and built for Harry Gillard.

Any list of Collings motor launches should be prefaced by the comments of Count Von Luckner, the German sea raider of World War I who tried to escape from New Zealand in the *Pearl* (built in 1912), after being interned on Motihue Island. He remarked about this launch: "I found the *Pearl* an excellent sea boat. If I should at any time need a boat for a similar purpose I hope one of yours is available."

Older Collings vessels include the *Paikea*, *Marguerite*, *Fleetwing*, and *Ruatangi*, and more recently the *Tamaroa* and *Makura*. Two Collings launches that have made notable voyages are *Ruamano*, a 13 m boat built for Alf Court (her maiden voyage in 1926 was 640 km around New Zealand), and *Frangipani* (built for Zane Grey, the noted American author and sportsman). Over 14 m long, she was built about 1930. Alex crewed on her delivery voyage of 3700 km from Auckland to Tahiti. Both of these boats were petrol-powered.

Collings speedboats achieved many successes, including the Masport Cup. The 6.4 m *Fleetwing* won the first New Zealand speedboat championship in 1914 — designed, built and driven by Charlie Collings.

In the early 1920s *Pussyfoot* held the open championship for several years. *Fleetwing Junior*, built in 1922, was one of the last of Charlie's champions. She was the first boat designed and built in this country to exceed 60 m.p.h. (96 km.p.h.). This boat was not merely a racer. In 1926 she made a run from Auckland to the Bay of Islands, including two short stops, in under four hours. The purpose of the trip was to inspect four new swordfish launches built by Collings that year and to interview Zane Grey in his yacht *Fisherman*.

Bonzo, built for Mr F. B. Cadman, was a sister ship to *Fleetwing* (except that she used a surface propeller). A third sister ship, *Kotuku*, went to Wanganui. She was powered by a 300 h.p. Fiat motor.

These boats were 7.9 m long by 2.6 m in beam. they were planked with two skins of kauri — an inner diagonal of 7.9 mm and a fore and aft of 11.1 mm — with oiled Egyptian cotton between and no caulking of the plank seams. They were closely ribbed. They were designed to be flexible; they didn't work or leak, even after many years of punishing racing.

Fleetwing was originally fitted with a Hall Scott, but this was replaced by a 200 h.p. Curtis which drove her at 45 knots. *Bonzo* also had the same size Curtis engine, but she was also equipped for cruising, with bunks, a toilet and two large tanks. *Fleetwing* was left empty.

Bonzo's surfacing propeller was 890 mm in diameter, with as much area in one blade as an underwater prop had in all three. Being fitted out for cruising, she was slower than the lighter *Fleetwing* — but she still reached 40 knots. These speeds were achieved on 1250 r.p.m., and were timed runs — no speedos were fitted in those days.

Surprise, for a long time the fastest whaler in New Zealand, was also built to the same design, although she was more heavily constructed. Two or three were built for Peranos of Picton. Some 11 m whale chasers that did 36 knots were also built.

About this time the firm was also building many notable outboard hulls, many of which were raced with considerable success by Charlie Collings. He built some to the American Blimp design, which was a popular single-step hydroplane. He used the four-cylinder Elto outboard for racing, and one of his best-known boats was called *Elto*.

Johnny Johnson of Auckland, who raced against Charlie Collings in those days, recalls winning the Auckland outboard championship with a Blimp that Collings and Bell had built him. "It was a boat with a fairly high deck and it was heavier than necessary for the class," said Mr Johnson. "So while Charlie was away down south doing a job on one of Zane Grey's launches Alex and I took all the superstructure off, replaced the deck with a piece of canvas and braced the hull with some well-placed pieces of conduit. It won the title."

Moose was a fast launch designed and built for Sir Noel Cole of Moose Lodge, Rotoiti. She was used by Queen Elizabeth and the Duke of Edinburgh when they stayed there.

The coming of World War II found Charlie too old to repeat his wartime services. But Alex certainly represented his family. In spite of indifferent health he was intimately concerned in the organising of the Naval Auxiliary Patrol and the Harbour and Gulf Defence Unit.

More important still was his part in organising and helping to operate United Ship and Boat Builders Ltd. and Associated Boat Builders Ltd. These companies were controlled by the United States armed services and made a valuable contribution to the Pacific war by co-ordinating and extending all the private shipbuilding facilities in Auckland.

Vessels launched included small tugs, general purpose vessels, powered lighters and fairmiles, some of which are still in operation as passenger vessels. (Fairmiles were large naval launches, built during World War II.) With the cessation of hostilities, Alex's professional skill was used by the Government in the disposing of the craft commandeered and built during the war.

The year 1946 saw the death of Charlie Collings and also the commencement of yacht building at the St. Mary's Bay yard. Vessels such as *Ngatiawa*, *Anthea II*, *Tamaroa* and *Makura* were launched from this yard, which finally closed when access to the sea was cut off by the road to the Auckland Harbour Bridge. From then on Alex spent more and more time at his drawing board designing small craft of all sorts.

These included *Tiakina*, built in England to be the pilot boat for the Wellington Harbour Board and steamed to that port; *Akarana*, a pilot boat built locally for the Auckland Harbour Board; *Manaia*, a 23 m 600 h.p. pilot boat for the Whangarei Harbour Board; *Deodar*, the Auckland police launch; three 17 m vessels designed and equipped for the Lepers Trust Board as small hospital vessels for the Solomon Islands; three Meteor-class fast launches designed specifically for fast tourist work on lakes and in the Bay of Islands; several small tugs and barges for working sand and shingle in inland waters.

On the drawing board at the time of his death was a steel trawler as well as a twin-screw vehicular ferry for operating in the Hokianga Harbour.

The record of club service by both Charles and Alex Collings is almost as impressive as their boatbuilding record.

Charlie Collings was commodore of the North Shore Sailing Club, an official of the Herne Bay Sailing Club, commodore of the New Zealand Power Boat Association, commodore of the Ponsonby Cruising Club and also an official of the Auckland Anniversary Regatta Committee.

Alex Collings was eight years secretary, two years chairman and eventually a life member of the Auckland Anniversary Regatta Committee, for several years secretary and later a life member of the Ponsonby Cruising Club, secretary for 23 years of the Auckland Yacht and Motor Boat Association (now the Auckland Yachting Association) and in addition was a member of the Royal New Zealand Yacht Squadron and several other clubs.

Alex Collings also taught naval architecture and boat building for 20 years at the Auckland Technical Institute. Mr John Brooke who was associated with him through these classes as well as through boating in general, says of him: "Alex was a mine of information on the mathematical side of yacht design, power requirements and propeller designs. In spite of his bluff exterior he would go to any length to do a good turn for a young apprentice or fellow boatbuilder. He was a kindly man with real creative ability."

Alexander John Collings died in November 1967. With his passing another link with the history of New Zealand boating was severed.

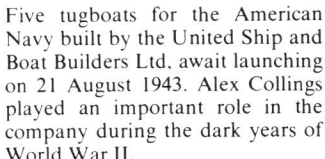
Five tugboats for the American Navy built by the United Ship and Boat Builders Ltd, await launching on 21 August 1943. Alex Collings played an important role in the company during the dark years of World War II.

8.

The House of Logan

TWO FAMILIES dominated yachting and indeed all pleasure boating in New Zealand from 1870 to 1930, and their influence is still felt in yacht construction and design today. In chapter three we discussed the Bailey family. Now it is the turn of the Scottish family Logan.

Robert Logan Senior, a native of Dumbarton, Scotland, arrived in Auckland with his family in 1874. After looking around the area for a place in which to settle and follow his craft, he decided in 1878 to reside in Devonport on Auckland's North Shore. He came to New Zealand a fully qualified yachtbuilder and designer, having served his apprenticeship with the famous Clyde shipbuilder William Steele. At the time of his emigration to New Zealand, Logan was actually managing a Clydeside shipyard. He brought with him to Auckland a knowledge of the sweet lines and fair curves of the famous designer Fife, under whom he had actually studied. This knowledge was obvious in the Auckland yachts Logan designed and built — they had the smart counter and graceful fiddle-bow that marked all Fife-designed vessels.

Logan's craftmanship actually preceded him to New Zealand, for James Logan (no relation) had earlier in 1871 imported from Scotland a smart little steamer called the *Eclipse*. This steamer, which was used on the Riverhead run in opposition to the *Gemini* owned by Captain Casey, was designed and build by Logan when he was managing the Steele yard on the Clyde. It is believed that this contact with New Zealand prompted Robert Logan to come to this country, thus enriching the ship and yachtbuilding industry.

Robert Logan Senior opened his Devonport yard in 1878, together with his sons John, Robert and Archibald. He operated there until 1895, when he transferred the business to the south side of the Harbour, close to the old Kauri Timber Company yards (burnt down in 1934) in Customs Street West. During this period at Devonport Logan and his sons were to earn a proud name throughout not only New Zealand but also Australia. The *New Zealand Herald* of the day described him as "one of the best yachtbuilders south of the line".

Robert Logan's arrival in Auckland coincided with the start of big yacht racing on the Waitemata. He was often heard to declare how the first sight of the Hauraki Gulf, the harbour and the numerous offshore islands led him to believe that he had come to a place that could only be described as a yachtsman's paradise.

The first yacht Logan designed and built in New Zealand was the *Sarita* for Mr George Niccol. This yacht was quickly followed by the *Lala* (three tonnes) for Mr A. Buchanan and the *Dandy* (five tonnes) for Mr Henry Niccol. These three yachts proved the equal of any on the harbour and quickly established Logan's reputation as the designer and builder of fast yachts.

At this time (the late 1870s) the Pacific Island trade with New Zealand had begun to be opened up. A large number of trading vessels were being built in Auckland, both for trading amongst the islands and also for carrying copra to Auckland. Robert Logan and his sons secured a large share of this shipbuilding, and his company was kept very busy with this commercial business — as well as continuing to design and build yachts.

A major assignment was the designing and building of a royal barge for the King of Tonga. This barge measured 11 m long by 2.4 m beam and 915 mm draft. It was diagonally planked, copper fastened and christened *Vuna*, after the first crown prince of Tonga. The vessel was furnished in a most luxuriant style, with a full-length awning supported on brass stanchions. Across the stern was emblazoned "Koe atua mo tonga ko noku tofia" ("God and Tonga — my inheritance"). At the same time the Tongan Government placed an order with Logan to build a copra-carrying ketch and a police cutter.

In 1880 Mr A. Buchanan, who had previously commissioned Logan to design and build *Lala*, placed an order for Logan to build *Lala II* (six tonnes). This yacht proved fast and able, but was no match for the original yacht which established Logan's reputation.

This was the famous 4.5 tonne cutter *Jessie Logan* (named after Logan's wife) which in her first 15 starts won 13 races and was second twice. The *Jessie Logan* was launched in January 1880 to the order of Mr Walter Jones, a well-known Auckland yachtsman of the time. In 1889 the old *Wellington Post* declared: "The *Jessie Logan* is unquestionably the prettiest, and we believe the fastest yacht of her size in the colony. She is wonderful for her speed and weatherly qualities. Her lines are beautiful." A great compliment indeed to Robert Logan and his sons.

The yacht's record still stands unbeaten: first, Auckland Regatta, 1880; defeated *Lala II* in a special match race, February 1880; first, Ponsonby Regatta, March 1880; first, Auckland Regatta, 1881; defeated *Joy* (the Bailey champion) in a match race, February 1881; second, Auckland Regatta, 1882; first, North Shore Regatta, November 1882; first, Auckland Regatta, 1883; first, Ponsonby Regatta, March 1883; second, Auckland Regatta, 1884; first, Auckland Regatta, 1885; first Auckland Regatta, 1886, 1887, 1888 and 1889.

For the owners of *Jessie Logan* competition in Auckland was becoming difficult to find — competing owners would simply not race against her. So the yacht was sailed to Wellington, where she won the Wellington Regatta in 1890 and again in 1894. Walter Jones had sold her in 1889 to Mr A. Dixon, and it was under this new ownership that she raced in Wellington. She was beaten only twice in Auckland — on both occasions by Logan-designed and built yachts. *Jessie Logan* never returned to Auckland; as recently as 1956 she was still afloat in Nelson, stripped of all her sailing gear and being used as a fishing boat.

To have designed and built the *Jessie Logan* would have represented the acme of achievement to many yacht designers, but it was only one of Robert Logan's claims to fame. In 1880 he built the well-known cutter *Daisy* for Mr S. Holland. This vessel was designed as a sailing-fishing boat, and she proved the undoubted champion of the Auckland fishing fleet for many years. Mr Walter Jones, who had previously owned *Jessie Logan*, then commis-

sioned the 7.62 m open yacht *Maggie* from the Logans. She was launched in January 1881, immediately winning her class in the Auckland Regatta of that year. Later that same year Mr W. Williams, a large fish merchant in Auckland, had the cutter *Christina* built; she proved a very fast yacht.

Logan was now well established. Mr J. L. R. Bloomfield, who was later commodore of the Royal New Zealand Yacht Squadron from 1894 to 1896 and who had the famous *Viking* built by the rival firm of Baileys, now commissioned Logan to build the *Arawa*. This yacht measured 11 m on the waterline and 2.3 m in the beam. In her first race, the North Shore Regatta in 1882, she beat both the *Rita*, the crack Bailey yacht at the time, and the *Christina*. At the 1882 Auckland Regatta she again beat the *Rita*. A special challenge race around Tiri Tiri Island and back (a distance of 48 km) was organised for the two yachts. The *Arawa* won by 17 and a half minutes, and the *Auckland Star* at the time commented: "Mr Logan now indisputably holds the proud position of being the designer and builder of the best yachts ever turned out of Auckland yards."

By this time, the two firms of Bailey and Logan controlled practically all the yachtbuilding business in New Zealand, and there was of course extremely keen competition between the rival families. A second challenge race around Tiri Tiri Island between the *Arawa* and *Rita* was again organised, and again the *Arawa* won soundly.

As a result of these successes, Mr C. H. Street, a well-known Auckland businessman, had Logan build a yacht to beat the *Arawa*. This was the *Muritai* (Maori for "sea breeze"), but for some reason Mr Street never rigged her for racing — in spite of the belief among the yachtsmen of Auckland that she was the fastest of all Logan's yachts.

Muritai was followed by the *Tawera* ("morning star"), of six and a half tonnes, built in 1884. She proved a fast yacht. In 1887 Mr C. B. Stone ordered the famous *Matangi*, which flew the commodore's flag of the Royal New Zealand Yacht Squadron in 1887-1888. At this time Mr Stone was commodore of this august club. *Matangi* had graceful but powerful lines, and her racing record was very impressive.

In 1893 Robert Logan designed and built a yacht which was classed as an "epoch maker" because of her then revolutionary wide beam

Perhaps the oldest sailing class in New Zealand. Royal New Zealand Navy Montague whalers racing on Auckland harbour. These boats developed from whaleboats still carrying a dipping lugsail rig.

and powerful midsection. All yachts up to this time were narrow beamed with great draft and were often quaintly called "planks on edge". This yacht was the five-rater *Aorere*, which raced in Auckland for many years with a great deal of success. It is pleasing to write that at the great age of 83 years *Aorere* is still afloat in Whangarei Harbour and is in good condition.

Another yacht built in the same year, this time by the Logan brothers without the supervision of "old master" Robert Logan, was the sweetly lined two and a half-rater *Gloriana*, named after a famous American racing yacht of the period. *Gloriana* was owned by the Logan brothers and raced for many years under their control, flying the famous black and white vertical striped racing pennant of the Logan family. Like the *Aorere*, *Gloriana* is still afloat on the Auckland harbour and is in extremely good condition, a great tribute to her builders and to her many owners over eight decades.

Robert Logan's talents were applied not only to yachts and trading vessels. His first love was certainly the creation of fast, seaworthy racing yachts, but he also built other types of boats. In the 1880s whaleboat racing was very popular in Auckland, and great interest and wagering took place, particularly on the result of the Auckland regatta championship. The specifications of these racing whaleboats varied greatly from the "real" whaleboat they evolved from. The length was not to exceed 10.6 m, beam not less than 1.2 m, depth not less than 483 mm at midship section, from top of keel to gunwale. The sheer was not to be less than 203 mm, the planking must be 7.9 mm kauri, and the timbers 6.3 x 19 mm at 203 mm centres. No batswings were al-

lowed, and the boats were to be rowed with five oars and steered with one oar.

At times prize money amounted to £100 per race, and crews from Hauraki, Waitemata, St. George, Manakau, Ponsonby and North Shore clubs competed. The Waitemata Club had a whaleboat built by Charles Bailey, and it proved unbeatable. The St. George Club called for tenders for a new boat, and when Robert Logan was announced as the successful tenderer, there was much scepticism from the whaleboat men: "Logan can build yachts, but whaleboats . . .". The boat's performance silenced all critics, for it beat everything. The *Auckland Star* commented: "Beyond doubt it is the prettiest and fastest whaleboat on the harbour, and does infinite credit to her designer and builder, Mr Logan." Soon each club owned a Logan whaleboat.

The building of yachts, whaleboats, island trading vessels and royal barges did not exhaust Logan's versatile genius. He built a number of steam launches, and designed and built the *Neptune* (30 tonnes) — a steamer for the Kaipara trade — the *Kawau* for the Coastal Steamship Co., the ferry steamer *Birkenhead* for the Northcote Ferry Co., and smart vessels such as the *Waimare*, *Taniwha*, *Kapanui*, *Kotiti* and *Tasman*, and an auxiliary schooner for the Governor of Samoa.

Robert Logan's yachts had success not only in New Zealand. One crossed the Tasman and beat Australian boats in their own waters. This yacht was, of course, the *Akarana* (the word is a Maori adaptation of "Auckland"), which Logan designed and built in late 1880 to race in the Melbourne Centennial Exhibition of 1881. *Akarana* was designed to rate at five tonnes, which under New Zealand rules she did exactly. But when she arrived in Australia and was measured by the Australians she was found to rate at 6.5 tonnes and therefore had to race in the "10 tonnes and under" class. In spite of being a lot smaller than other entrants in this class, she won the first prize money of £140. Because of this success she was invited by the St. Kilda yacht club to participate in the club's championship race, which she won. It was an extremely good effort from the first New Zealand yacht to take part in international competition. *Akarana* represented not only New Zealand, but also the Auckland Yacht Club (renamed the Royal New Zealand Yacht Squadron in 1902) which sponsored her at the Melbourne regatta.

Akarana was then sailed to Sydney, and in

that city's anniversary regatta of 1881 won the "20 tonne and under" class, defeating the Sydney champion *Sirocco*. This latter yacht was later to achieve fame when the movie actor Errol Flynn sailed her to New Guinea.

In Sydney *Akarana* was sold to a local businessman, Mr H. Abrahams, who used her for many years on Sydney Harbour. *Akarana* is still afloat on Sydney Harbour, and is said to be the oldest yacht still afloat in Australasian waters.

The last two yachts the Logans built at their yard in Devonport were the 11 m *Rarere* and the very well-known cutter *Waitangi*, which was destined to fly the commodore's pennant of the Royal New Zealand Yacht Squadron no less than four times: from 1920 to 1922 for Mr J. B. Johnston, from 1922 to 1924 for Mr A. Burt, from 1926 to 1928 for Mr J. W. Frater and from 1932 to 1934 for Mr J. H. Frater.

Only the *Ariki* has ever achieved anything like this proud record.

Many other yachts were built by Robert Logan and his sons at Devonport between 1878 and 1895, but those we have discussed are the ones which really established this Scottish family as the most successful boatbuilders in Australasia in this period. Robert Logan certainly vindicated his statement in a letter to his old employer William Steele in Scotland when he wrote in 1878, on the eve of opening his own yard: "I hope to make a good name for myself." Today, a century later, that good name still lives on.

Although the three-skin diagonal principle was already known when Robert Logan Senior arrived in New Zealand, it is safe to say that he was the man who was primarily responsible for first using this method in the construction of racing yachts. The proof that this method was a sound one is ably demonstrated in the yachts he and his sons built; the *Aorere*, *Gloriana*, *Ariki*, *Rainbow* and *Rawhiti*, all at least 70 years old, are still afloat and in active service.

In 1895 Robert Logan Senior transferred his yard across the harbour from Devonport to where the Auckland city markets are now sited. However in 1894 his sons had left the employ of their father and established the business known as Logan Brothers, in Quay Street on the Railway Wharf (now of course demolished). The Logan Brothers partnership, — John, Robert and Archibald — very quickly built up a reputation that rivalled that of their illustrious father.

In the twilight of his life Robert Logan Senior

The steel cutter, *Thetis*, built by Seager Brothers, and owned by Val Masefield, drying gear off Motutapu Island, after a race in 1904. In the background *Moana* does the same. *Moana* built in 1895, is still afloat today.

did not build any more fast racing yachts, but concerned himself with yacht repairs and upkeep and a limited amount of commercial shipbuilding. In 1919 he passed away, leaving behind him perhaps the finest reputation in the Southern Hemisphere as the creator and builder of beautiful racing yachts. With each year that passes, the memory of this humble Scottish boatbuilder becomes less clear and it is essential that the importance of this great man's work to not only the history of New Zealand yachting but also the overall development of manufacturing in this country is recorded for future generations.

Although Robert Logan's sons commenced building under the name of Logan Brothers, they probably never supplanted the reputation and esteem of their father in the eyes of the public. Still, there is no question that the repu-

tation they established in the 16 years the partnership lasted represents a similarly splendid record.

In the late nineties yacht-designing had undergone a transition, represented by a comparison between the little *Gloriana* (1892) with the beautiful cutter *Rainbow* (1898). The latter had what by today's standards one might term a "modern" hull form. This change in form can be traced to George Watson's masterpiece, the royal yacht *Britannia*. Ever in line with the latest ideas in yacht design, Logan Brothers were soon incorporating this new hull form in their own vessels, to the extent that one might say that the old ideas died with the birth of the little *Gloriana*. Fast boat that she was, she could not match a boat such as the *Queenie*, for instance, which was designed on the *Britannia* formula.

It is impossible to record every yacht turned out by Logan Brothers. The space required would fill a volume, so I will touch at random on some of the more well-known vessels which were constructed in their yard. *Gloriana*, a two and a half-rater, has a long and successful career as a racer; she won the Ponsonby regattas in 1892 and 1894, the Judge's Bay regattas in 1892, 1894 and 1895, and also the Auckland Yacht Club races in 1893, 1894 and 1895. The five-rater *Moana*, built for the Wilson brothers, was a fine model. She carried off the prizes in her class at the Ponsonby and Auckland regattas in 1896 and 1897, and has been a consistent performer since then. *Mahaki*, a two and a half-rater built for Messrs Chatfield and Moore, also bears a long and successful record. These three cutters are still in first class order, *Moana* in particular being excellently preserved. She now sails under a Bermudian rig.

Perhaps one of the finest yachts built in the early days of the partnership Logan brothers was the 10-rater *Thelma*. At the time of her launching she possessed a speed and seaworthiness unrivalled by other Auckland keelers. She was for many years owned by the redoubtable J. L. R. Bloomfield, who had previously owned the *Viking*. *Thelma* carried his pennant as commodore of the Royal New Zealand Yacht Squadron from 1907 to 1918. Just prior to the outbreak of World War II she was sailed to

Right: An historic photograph of *Rainbow* taken as she runs through the Motikue Passage in 1956 carrying her modern Bermuda rig and a tremendous area of sail. Leo Bouzaid at the helm.

Rainbow's crew take it easy during a calm period on a trip to Kawau Island in 1903.

A 1901 photograph of the mighty *Rainbow*, considered by many old yachtsmen to be the Logan masterpiece.

The fast C-class cutter *Queenie*. She still sails on the Auckland harbour, today with a lofty Bermuda rig.

Tahiti, where she remained for some years. In 1948 she was purchased by the United States Navy and sailed to Honolulu, where she was thoroughly overhauled. Today *Thelma* sails in Hawaiian waters as an officers' recreational yacht.

The three Logan brothers never had the most harmonious of relationships, but each had inherited the skill of their father. Robert Junior looked after the office, while John and Archibald were the shipwrights (although each worked on different sides of the shed). A total of five apprentices were employed. It was during this period that the designing skills of Archie became apparent — his responsibility was setting out the drawings full size on the floor and running out his curves with battens and chalk.

In this way the lines of the yacht which perhaps has had the greatest impact on New Zealand yachting was laid out and built. This was the famous cutter *Rainbow*, built in 1898 for Mr A. T. Pittar. *Rainbow* measured 15.2 m overall, 10.3 m on the waterline, 2.6 m in beam and had a draft of 2 m. Her design was influenced by the Scottish genius George Watson, whom we discussed earlier. Watson's royal yacht *Britannia* was the first yacht to incorporate the spoon-bow and full midsection. No more clipper-bow, narrow-beam, slack midsection yachts were ever again built in New Zealand.

With the exception of the big cutter *Ilex*, built in 1902 by the Logans (she had a clipper bow but a powerful midsection), no more clipper bows with their graceful fiddles were designed until there was a brief nostalgia boom with fibreglass Herreshoff designs in the late 1960s.

Rainbow proved a champion, beating everything on Auckland harbour and even on Sydney harbour (where she was sailed in 1900). Sixty years later, owned by the late Leo Bouzaid (father of One-Ton Cup champion Chris), she was still capable of giving modern fliers such as *Ranger* a close, hard race. *Rainbow* passed through several hands until she was purchased by Arch Buchanan, who reduced her rig for cruising. In November 1937 she was purchased by the partnership of Messrs J. Patrick and F. Cloke, who previously owned the Charles Bailey-built C-class cutter *Speedwell*. Patrick and Cloke rerigged her with a lofty Bermudian rig and raced her hard with the Royal New Zealand Yacht Squadron. They in turn sold her to Leo Bouzaid in the late 1940s. Under his ownership she achieved considerable success, and it is sad to relate that Bouzaid died while at the helm. *Rainbow* was sold out of the racing fleet to a new owner in Nelson, where she is still located today.

Following the *Rainbow* came her smaller sister, the very well performed *Queenie*. Launched in 1903, she is still afloat and winning races. In fact 70 years after her launching her lines so appealed to an American yachtsman that he proposed to ship her to California. This never eventuated and the *Queenie* still sails the waters of the Hauraki Gulf.

A year later, in 1904, came the yacht many yachtsmen regarded as the most powerful design ever produced by the Logan brothers. This yacht is, of course, the beautiful *Ariki* (which means in Maori "leader" or "chief"). Since her launching 72 years ago she has repeatedly led the first division of the Auckland keeler fleet. In fact up to 1938 she was the acknowledged Auckland champion. (In 1938 the re-commissioned *Rainbow* and the newly launched *Ranger*, the latter having a lofty Bermuda rig, displaced the old champion.)

The *Ariki* measures 16.4 m overall, 11.6 m on the waterline, 3.3 m in beam and draws 2.1 m of water. She is unique in the Auckland keeler fleet in that she is the only gaff-rigged yacht which still sets a topsail when the conditions are suited. She therefore attracts just as much interest on

The Logan brothers' masterpiece *Rawhiti* reaching fast under yankee jib and staysail in the Waiheke Passage during a R.N.Z.Y.S. race to Te Kouma in 1958.

the harbour today as when she was launched.

Like other Logan yachts, *Ariki* has proudly carried the commodore's pennant of the Royal New Zealand Yacht Squadron no less than four times, first in 1918 for Mr E. C. Blomfield, again in 1930 for Mr N. Macky, in 1955 for Mr A. A. Angell, and in 1976 for Mr H. Littler.

Plans have been put forward to present the old champion to the yacht squadron as a sail training vessel. This would be most appropriate, because the *Ariki* is not only the only first division keeler to retain her gaff rig; she also is the only yacht of this type not to be structurally altered. She still has long flush decks, broken only by hatchways and skylights, and is totally devoid of modern appliances such as winches and of electronic gadgetry. *Ariki* remains a graceful tribute not only to the Logans but also to a peaceful age 70 years ago, when New Zealand was young and free from the tensions of the present period.

Ariki was quickly followed by the 16.5 m *Rawhiti* (in Maori "the east"), built for the tireless A. T. Pittar (who of course had *Rainbow* built seven years earlier). Mr Pittar, who had emigrated to Sydney, ordered from the Logans "another and better *Rainbow*". What he got was

The superb cutter *Ariki* reaching down the Auckland harbour under full sail. She is flying the famous black and white horizontal racing pennant of the Logan brothers. *Ariki* is today the last large gaff-rigged cutter in New Zealand.

54

exactly that: 16.5 m overall, 11.9 m on the waterline and 2.9 m in beam. *Rawhiti* was sailed to Sydney under jury rig, and for the next 30 years was the undisputed champion of Sydney Harbour. Her second owner was Frank Albert, the well-known music publisher. When larger yachts were challenging *Rawhiti's* record in the 1930s he laid her up, until 1946. She was then purchased by Mr S. E. Marler of Auckland. A condition of sale was that *Rawhiti* must not race in Australia, but must return to Auckland. This she did, arriving back in Auckland on 29 December 1946 after an absence of 41 years.

Rawhiti sailed in the first division fleet of the yacht squadron, winning the coveted points prize in 1957; in 1967 she carried the commodore's pennant of Mr B. M. Marler, son of the man who bought her in Sydney. In the early 1970s *Rawhiti* suffered the fate of so many of the lovely old cutters. Rerigged with metal spars as a sloop, the lovely graceful counter removed and replaced with an ugly retroussé stern, the cabintop built up and a dog house added, the *Rawhiti* today is hard to recognise as a Logan brothers' masterpiece.

Another large cutter built by the Logan brothers was the *Ilex* launched in 1902. She was notable for being the only clipper-bowed yacht built by the Logans after the debut of *Rainbow* in 1898. *Ilex* achieved considerable publicity in 1961 when, renamed the *Tuaikaepau*, she was lost on Minerva Reef on a voyage from Tonga to Auckland carrying illegal immigrants. This wreck, and the subsequent privations of the stranded Tongans on the reef before being found by searching planes of the Royal New Zealand Air Force, attracted worldwide interest.

The fame and skill of the Logans spread through both the Australian and South African yachting worlds. For example, several small yachts of the "patiki" type were built and shipped to South Africa. At Port Elizabeth in the years 1906 to 1913 the Logan "patikis" *Ibis*, *Shingana*, and *Nancy* won many first prizes. From the South African *Cape Times* comes the following 1911 extract from a portion of a speech made by a South African yachtsman at a gathering in the Royal Hotel after the Lipton Cup finals had been sailed and won by the Logan-designed *Tess* of the Durban Yacht Club:

"We came here to beat you fairly and squarely. That we have succeeded is a source of great gratification to us. Whether we deserved to win is another matter. We got the best designer in the Southern Hemisphere to design the boat, and the best colonial workman in Durban to build her."

Such was the fine tribute paid to the Logan brothers, designers of the *Tess*.

So the fame of the Logans spread to many countries — New Zealand, Australia and South Africa, and also to the Pacific. Their work was also followed by friends and associates in England and Scotland. In 1917 the editor of the English journal *The Yachting Monthly* wrote at some length of the outstanding successes of the Logans. "Logan Senior hailed from the Clyde," he said, "and from there he carried to Auckland the sweet lines and fair curves of the Fife firm." Speaking of the old *Waitangi* he wrote: "She made the voyage from her birthplace to Wellington in six days and 18 hours — a remarkable passage." On this occasion *Waitangi* was sailed by Logan Senior. It should of course be mentioned that besides designing and building yachts, the Logans were also keen yachtsmen, sailing many of their boats to victory.

In 1910 the partnership of Logan Brothers was dissolved, not because of disharmony amongst the brothers but because their yard was required for the rebuilding of the Kings Wharf power station. (It is understood that £8000 was paid to the Logans for the unexpired portion of the lease.) The last yacht built by the Logan brothers was the *Rawene*, which was launched in 1909. She is today still in her original condition, beautifully maintained by the Gifford family.

The brothers went their various ways, retaining an interest in yachting. But only Archibald continued actively building and designing fast and seaworthy yachts and launches. He moved to Stanley Point in Devonport; at the back of his house on a section which ran down to the waters of Ngataringa Bay he built a shed in which were built some of Auckland's fastest centreboard yachts.

On his retirement Arch Logan severed his connection with boatbuilding, but he never gave up his work as a designer. Periodically he was approached and asked to design a new craft. Possessing the versatility of his father, he would draw up a plan to meet the prospective owner's requirements.

Although the Logan brothers will always be best remembered for their fine racing yachts, they did not confine their whole attention to these craft. Like their father before them they

The K-class *Waiomo* built by Bill Couldrey in 1938, runs "downhill" in the Hauraki Gulf during a R.N.Z.Y.S. race.

Following the adoption of the M-class by the Royal New Zealand Yacht Squadron, Arch Logan was asked to design a small class racer about 3.6 m long. The result was the very pretty little Silver Fern class, in reality a scaled down M-class. It enjoyed great popularity in the 1940s and 1950s, but like other classes such as T, X and Y it died out in the 1960s with the advent of plywood and fibreglass building materials.

But Arch Logan did not confine his abilities to small yachts. He designed the mullet boats *Omatere* (7.9 m), the 6.70 m yachts *Valeria*, *Marika* and *Rakoa*, and the square bilge *Surprise* and *Alerte* (5.5 m). In 1935 he designed the *Little Jim* to replace a yacht of the same name wrecked on Great Barrier Island on Christmas Day 1933. This new yacht was built by Bill Couldrey at Northcote and proved a champion from her very first race.

The launching of *Little Jim* started a spate of first class yachtbuilding. From 1935 to 1940 no less than eight first class yachts were launched. Of these, four were designed by Arch Logan, a great tribute to this son of a Scottish immigrant.

These four yachts were the *Aramoana*, *Gypsy* and *Waiomo* (all built by Bill Couldrey) and the *Tarawera*. *Aramoana* was the second division champion for many years, while the *Gypsy* attracted a great deal of interest. She was launched in 1939 as a gaff-rigged topsail cutter, the last yacht to be built with this rig in Auckland. Together with *Waiomo* she was reregistered in the 1950s to race with the K-class and the gaff rig was replaced with the modern Bermuda rig. The *Waiomo* was for many years owned by Mr Justice Speight, who flew the commodore's pennant of the Royal New Zealand Yacht Squadron from her during his tenure in office from 1961 to 1963. The *Tawera* was built by Colin Wild at Stanley Bay.

The other yachts launched at this time were the *Tamatea*, designed by expatriate New Zealander Arthur Robb, *Matia*, designed and built by the Lidgard Brothers, *Ngataringa*, designed and built by Colin Wild, and the mighty *Ranger*, designed and built by the Tercel brothers of Ponsonby in 1938.

Archibald Logan died on 27 March 1940. His brother James died in 1939, while William, the last of the partnership, passed away in 1955. Archie Logan left two sons, one of whom was killed during World War II. His younger son Jack achieved a great deal of success racing yachts of 5.5 m in the period 1946 to 1955.

were engaged in designing and building almost any class of vessel.

Some years after Arch Logan retired he designed and built the first of what was to prove in later years a most popular type of small racing yacht. With the new M-class he again proved his skill as a designer. After a member of the Royal New Zealand Yacht Squadron had taken out one of these boats to try her out, he was so enthusiastic over her performances that he told Mr Logan he would like to have them adopted by the squadron. They were adopted, and the class soon grew into a fine racing fleet of restricted 5.5 m Patikis.

The first of these was the straight-stemmed, sweetly lined *Matara*, which Arch Logan designed and built at Devonport with the help of his sons in 1939. He originally intended it to sail in the ill-fated world 18-footer (5.5 m) championship planned to be part of the Auckland Centennial Regatta of 1940. Due to war this was cancelled. *Matara*, which was Arch Logan's last design, was not destined to race until the end of hostilities in 1945. Meanwhile Archibald Logan had of course died and never saw his last creation sail.

However sailed by Jack Logan she proved a champion. She was finally sold to a Napier yachtsman. Jack then designed and built the controversial but extremely fast spoon-bowed 5.5 m *Komutu* and *Tarua*.

Jack Logan has continued the family boatbuilding tradition, working for many years for the late Brin Wilson. A little Logan magic still exists in modern Wilson-built yachts such as *Pathfinder*, *Rebel* and *Quicksilver*.

Arch Logan's *Little Jim* (nearest camera on the right) slogging up Rangitoto Channel with Auckland first division keelers in 1960. The launching of *Little Jim* signalled a spate of yachtbuilding.

9.

The square bilge yachts

NEARLY 60 YEARS AGO a Wellington yachtsman arrived in Auckland and saw for the first time the waters of the Waitemata Harbour. Born and bred in the more sombre surroundings and rigid climatic conditions of the southern city, where snug anchorages and extensive cruising grounds are unknown, he was immediately struck with the beauty and peaceful aspect of Auckland's incomparable gulf. Slowly his eyes took in the wide, curving beaches, the many islands dotting the water outside the harbour entrance, and away in the distance the hazy blue outlines of Great Barrier Island and the stately Coromandel Range. Thereafter two thoughts were uppermost in his mind: that Auckland possessed one of the finest cruising grounds in the world — and that there were very few small yachts. He realised that conditions in the innumerable shallow bays, tidal creeks and broad sea reaches of the harbour and gulf were ideal for safe cruising in a shoal-draught yacht, and so George Honour, the father of the square bilge boat, took upon himself the task of creating a suitable craft.

With half a lifetime of yachting experience acquired in Wellington behind him, he carefully studied the situation from every angle until he finally came to a decision. He would build the first of what he hoped would be a growing class, but the boat must have at least three qualifications: first, ease of construction for the amateur builder; second, low cost for the man of moderate means; and last, but by no means least, speed. The classes which were developed and increased year by year to the outbreak of World War II bear out faithfully all that was asked of the first boat.

So we learn that in 1918, after carrying out numerous experiments with drawings and models, George Honour was at last satisfied that he had evolved the right type of craft. In a ramshackle wood and iron shed on a spit of land running out into Hobson Bay, he set to work.

Out of the pile of kauri timber rose his first creation. At last she was completed. Standing amidst the shavings, resplendent in shining paint and varnish, the forerunner of Auckland's popular square bilge craft stood ready for the water.

News of a new boat travels fast amongst the yachting fraternity and soon the little shed was the centre of Auckland's armchair critics. Wise yachtsmen came to view the new yacht. From her rockered keel to the neatly capped coamings, inside and out, they looked her over and, muttering to themselves, they went away convinced that they had seen the birth of the world's greatest freak.

What they actually did see was this: a straight-sided craft, 4.3 m overall, 1.7 m in beam, half-decked, with a narrow centreboard trunk. It was the bottom which caused the greatest comment. From aft, the keel ran in a fine sweeping curve until forward of amidships, where it rockered sharply upwards to meet a short, stubby stem post. Her floors rose quickly from the bow to aft of amidships, where they gradually flattened out to almost nothing at the broad tuck stern. Her construction was so light that two men could lift her off the stocks.

Gone was the craft which was then known as a "flattie", with a straight keel, wedge-shaped bottom and cumbersome construction. The critics felt this boat was so entirely different she simply could not be a success. But they were all wrong, and very soon realised their mistake.

Launching day saw the little yacht christened *Sasanof*, after that year's winner of the Melbourne Cup horse race. When she was launched she lay light as a feather on the surface, with her high chine showing above all round. When a gust of wind caught her, she blew over the water light as a piece of thistledown. Therein lay the success of this latest type of small sailing craft. In place of the former heavy vee-bottom boats of clumsy construction, George Honour reversed

The classic George Honour square bilge yacht. This is the *Millicent* (later to become *Sun*) built by Honour in 1922. Note the original gaff rig and cotton mainsail with vertical cloths and no battens. She is currently owned by the author.

the whole procedure by forming the bottom of the *Sasanof* much after the shape of a saucer, thus cutting weight down to a minimum. This loss in weight did not by any means weaken the boat, for the whole structure was well tied together with side seams battened. The floor was well fastened to solid frames, with steam-bent timbers between.

George Honour was only an amateur, but it was a pleasure to watch him at work on one of his numerous boatbuilding jobs. Early in his life he acquired the same idea as the old Dutch shipwrights — he always put a curve or rounded edge wherever he possibly could. For instance, he would never tolerate merely quickly running his plane along the edge of a piece of wood to take the corner off — that would not do at all. He carefully put a half-round, or full round, on every piece of wood that tied his boats together inside. The floors, timbers, bulkhead edges, locker door edges, hanging knees, seam battens, breast-hooks, quarter knees, dinghy seats and rowlock chocks were all sweetly curved and beautifully rounded over.

George Honour was often asked why he went to this trouble. He replied: "It looks nice. Curves are much more pleasing to the eye than ugly corners and edges. But that's not the only reason why I spend such a lot of time doing this extra work. You know how it hurts every time you knock yourself on a piece of square furniture; well you can never knock your elbows about in one of my boats. Another thing, it's next to impossible to keep paint or varnish on a corner or sharp edge; but rounded over, paint stays just as long as it does on a broad, flat surface. It's one of the things I could never understand why furniture builders started off on the wrong tack by making everything square and ugly-looking."

He was quite right, and an Honour boat could always be identified by this one small feature. It was not the only feature of his work that took the eye — his rivetting was a work of art. And inside yachts 5.5 m or over George applied no paint; everything was finished "bright", the timber being oiled or lightly varnished. It gave a most attractive appearance. The late Brin Wilson also finished the interior of the many fine yachts he built in this fashion. It is not only attractive but very practical.

George rigged his first boat with a high peaked gaff mainsail and jib, and as soon as he hauled *Sasanof* on the wind he knew she was fast. In a hard breeze she beat out to windward like a half-rater, and off the wind, with her spinnaker set in a short, choppy sea, the little craft literally rose out of the water and planed on her broad after section.

So the first milestone in the history of the square bilge yachts was passed, but George was not content to rest on his laurels. He soon found a buyer for *Sasanof* and immediately set about building his second boat, which he named *Sea Sprite*. From the lessons learned from studying the actions of his first yacht under sail, he built a still faster craft.

In spite of the adverse criticism which George Honour had suffered at the hands of a number of people, he managed to satisfy a small circle of far-sighted yachtsmen that here at last was one of the finest types of small craft they had ever seen. *Sea Sprite* had no sooner proved her superiority over her predecessor than she was sold, and George started work on his third boat, which he named *Sea Spook*.

By this time a number of square bilge enthusiasts were determined to try their hand at building a boat for their own use. Simultaneously with the building of *Sea Spook* no fewer than four other new boats, all built by amateurs off *Sea Spook* plans, were taking shape, namely *Sea Nymph*, *Sea Elf*, *Sea Imp* and *Continuance*. The next year saw the class growing by leaps and bounds; the following boats, built by amateurs (with but one exception) took to the water: *Sea Breeze*, *Early Dawn*, *Sea De'il*, *Sea Lion*, *Sea Bubble*, *Phyllis H*, *Sea Pixie* and *Whiz Bang*, the last-named being built by Colin Wild.

One can well understand that it was with pride and satisfaction that George Honour watched the steady growth of the square bilge yachts which all had their beginning in the little *Sasanof*. But in spite of the fact that the boats were increasing steadily in number and had more than proved themselves as a fast type of racing yacht, all endeavours on George's part to have the class adopted by the various Auckland yacht clubs were met by almost hostile refusal. In vain he tried to convince the chairmen and committees of various clubs that the 4.3 m square bilge was a good type of racing yacht to compete in their club fixtures. They would have nothing to do with them, and it may be recorded that a chairman of one club even went so far as to ask George when he intended to stop pestering them with requests for their adoption.

Although they were not permitted to race in registered yacht club fixtures there was nothing to prevent followers of the craft racing the boats amongst themselves. The early history of these craft includes many an exciting private match sailed for a small sweepstake. Actually the first recorded race by one of the 4.3 m square bilge boats took place in 1919. It was sailed between *Sea Sprite* and *Caprice*, the former winning the match.

In 1920 the Victoria Cruising Club realised that this ridiculous state of affairs could not last indefinitely. It decided to adopt the square bilge as a racing unit. And so, at long last, the boats came into their own.

We now come to the last of the 4.3 m boats built by George Honour before he turned his attention to a larger craft of the same type. In *Sea Gnome* he reached the peak of his fame in 4.3 m racing craft. She was champion of champions when he sold her, and thus severed his connection with the 4.3 m size. But he left behind him a wonderful racing record which will probably never be surpassed in this particular type of yacht. He was not only an amateur yachtbuilder; he was also one of the cleverest amateur skippers, sailing all his boats to victory, one after the other, as they were built. Through his keenness and untiring efforts he put the class on a most substantial footing. From the day of their adoption by the Victoria Cruising Club 4.3 m square bilge racing became increasingly popular each season on the Waitemata.

In 1922 George Honour laid the keel of the first of what was to prove in later years one of the most popular racing and cruising craft in Auckland, namely the 5.5 m (18 ft) unrestricted V-class yachts. His first was the *Wizard*, and although the general shape of the 4.3 m craft was still retained in the larger craft, many improvements came about with her building. She was not only designed for racing, but was also fitted out for coastwise cruising.

The boat had a comfortable little cabin under her deckhouse, with built-in berths, water tanks, locker space and facilities for cooking food when away cruising. The wooden dagger centreboard, which was almost universal in the 4.3 m craft, was exchanged for an iron plate swinging on a kingbolt. She carried a substantial gaff rig on her well stayed mast. There was no less than 31 sq m of canvas in her working mainsail and jib, while a masthead spinnaker brought her total sail area up to something like 46 sq m. No ballast was carried inside, the boat relying on her own stability (aided by a crew of three of four men to keep her on her feet in hard weather).

As the *Wizard* was being built, George set up

Another shot of the *Millicent*, later to become the *Sun*. Here she reaches up the Waitemata Harbour in January 1931.

the keel of another, named *Millicent*. This latter yacht, whose name was later changed to *Sun*, was, from the frame stage, built entirely by her owner. The *Wizard* proved to be a very fast type of yacht, and after racing her successfully in the 1922-23 season under the auspices of the Akarana Yacht Club, George sold her to a Mr E. Dalton. She was eventually sold to Messrs Smith and Parkinson of Tauranga, who after sailing her 194 km to this port raced her with considerable success.

After selling the *Wizard*, George at once commenced building again, and in quick succession two more of the 5.5 m craft, the *Magic* and the *Mystic*, were constructed and sold. These three yachts, and the *Millicent* too, achieved splendid racing records. Although the 4.3 m craft had a big following for many years, the 5.5 m boats of various types and shapes are now the most popular class. Both the *Sun* and the *Magic* are still afloat on Auckland harbour. The *Sun*, in particular, is in good condition, still retaining the original gaff rig she was launched with back in 1922. She is currently owned by the author.

Honour incorporated many novel ideas in the equipment of his yachts. Lightness with strength was the keynote of all his work, and this, combined with finely-cut sails, was in many ways responsible for the great success of all his boats. He was always a great believer in the roller reefing gear which he put on all his yachts' mainsails; he maintained that he repeatedly proved the great advantage this time-saving device has on a small racing craft, compared with the reef point method for shortening down. While racing he frequently shortened down without even coming up into the wind. He merely slacked away his main halyards while working the ratchet handle on the boom gear. Valuable time was thus saved, and often this means winning a race from other yachts which are staggering along under too much canvas.

Perhaps one of the most important innovations introduced in his craft was what is now known as "the shifting centreboard". Any yachtsman who has sailed a small craft possessing a dagger plate knows that shifting it slightly forward or aft in the centreboard trunk greatly assists the boat's performance when crosshauled on the wind. With this in mind, George eventually discarded the kingbolt method in his boats of 5.5 m and over, and adopted the shifting centreboard. When assembling the bottom planks in the centreboard trunk, he screwed a narrow gunmetal track, low down and inside each piece of timber. Where normally a hole for the orthodox kingbolt would be bored in the iron plate, George had a small round metal plug welded, so that it protruded about 6 mm on either side. These two metal shoulders slide on the gunmetal tracks, and allow the centreboard to rest in any desired position, either forward or aft when the plate is lowered down. The advantages of this shifting plate will be readily appreciated by those yachtsmen who have raced in this type of craft, for broadly speaking the lateral resistance may be altered at will to meet various conditions of windward sailing.

After sailing his various 5.5 m boats to many victories over a period of several years, George Honour severed his connections with these racing yachts and built the boat which he owned for many years. This craft, named *Mirage*, measured 6.7 m (22 ft) overall, and is merely a larger boat of the same type as the 5.5 m craft. She was beautifully put together, and during the many years he owned her George cruised hundreds of kilometres each summer, visiting the various seaside resorts and sailing offshore as far as the Great Barrier Island. Although she was a fast and seaworthy type, the 6.7 m square bilge class did not become popular. *Mirage* will consequently never have the opportunity of building up the notable racing record of her predecessors in the smaller classes.

With the exception of one craft of 4.3 m built at Paremata and two of 5.5 m, built in Auckland George Honour gave up his work as an amateur boatbuilder until 1938, when he constructed the 5.5 m *Miracle*. This craft was built for the express purpose of contesting the title for the "world's champion 18-footer (5.5 m)", the races being held in Auckland in February 1939.

In the *Miracle* George Honour made a radical change from his other boats, building her with what he calls a "shovel nose". This was one of the latest experiments in chine yachts. Instead of the chine log following the usual course from tuck to bow, it was lifted up abruptly by way of the main chainplates and connected to a rounded apron in place of the orthodox stem. A 4.3 m yacht named the *Impudence* had already been constructed on somewhat similar lines by the Highet brothers, who sailed her with considerable success for a number of seasons in Wellington and Paremata until she was sold to an Auckland yachtsman. They even took the boat to Tasmania and raced her with success in the centennial regatta held in February 1938. In view of the success of this boat, great hopes centred round the *Miracle*; her launching day was eagerly looked forward to by a number of interested yachtsmen. It is therefore regrettable to have to record that the new boat did not come up to expectations, and at no time during the championship races did she gain a place.

Yet one cannot help but admire George Honour for his ambitious attempt to introduce a new and hopefully phenomenally fast yacht. The *Miracle* was the last yacht built by this originator of the square bilge craft, all of which had their beginning in the little *Sasanof*. The hundreds of yachtsmen who sail this type of vessel should remember the services rendered by George Honour. In the face of hostile criticism and open ridicule at the hands of a number of people he carried on and nobly completed the difficult task of putting the class on a firm footing.

Many an amateur builder of long ago has cause to remember him, for George was always ready to help and advise in the planning, setting up and building of a new boat.

That the boats are fast and weatherly has been proved on many occasions. An example of this is the notable run made by the 5.5 m *Mystic* many years ago. Sailing in the Akarana Yacht Club's race to Awaroa Bay, she covered the course of 25 km in a few minutes under two hours, surely a splendid performance.

George Honour's own boat, the *Mirage*, is also a very fast and weatherly yacht, and is still in good condition on Auckland harbour. There is a little incident that once occurred on board this craft which is worthy of mention. While away on a Christmas cruise some seasons ago she was making a passage from Kawau Island to Cowes Bay on Waiheke Island. The yacht was running at the time under whole mainsail and spinnaker in a fresh breeze and on a choppy sea. Her crew, with the exception of one member who was lying asleep in his bunk, were all in the cockpit enjoying the warm sunshine which is always most pleasant in a vessel sailing off wind. Suddenly an extra heavy gust of wind came down on the yacht, and she started to run at greatly increased speed. A heavy pounding underneath the bottom of the boat caused the crew to look at one another in surprise. Alas for the poor sleeper! He awoke in great consternation and bounded out into the cockpit, convinced that the yacht was hitting bottom in shoal water. The smiles of his companions hastily reassured him that all was well, but he was equally amazed when he learned the cause of the terrific hammering that was going on underneath the *Mirage*. Lifting a dead weight of something like a tonne and a half, the pressure of the wind in the sails had brought the vessel out onto the surface, until she had started to plane at tremendous speed over the tops of the short seas. The performance of a ballasted boat coming to the surface and planing must surely be without parallel in the history of Auckland yachting. The Stewart 34 *Patari* owned by Lloyd Brookbanks once underwent a similar experience when racing in the Duder Cup race of 1969 (also running in a south-west gale). On that occasion she planed from the Compass Dolphin to Bean Rock.

The square bilge yachts still have a following in Auckland today, many amateur designers having contributed in building up a large fleet of 4.3 m and 5.5 m craft — although it is some years since one was launched. Among other amateur yachtsmen who have built fast boats on the chine principle may be mentioned Mr "Trott"

Willets, who constructed an early champion of the Waitemata and Manukau harbours, the 4.3 m *Cupid*, and the champion 5.5 m *Drone*, which he designed for the Curry brothers who built her. Becoming interested in the class, the Curry brothers turned their attention to more building, constructing the champions *Raider* and *Swallow*. In later years, another well-known amateur designer, Mr J. Brooke, designed a number of fast yachts including *Mania, Avenger, Muimai* and *Motare*.

With the advent of any new type of yacht it is only natural that designers are eager to improve on existing boats. Quite early in the history of the square bilge, radical changes were incorporated in the new craft — mainly in the underwater sections. So in opposition to the saucer-shaped bottom of the original type evolved by George Honour, we find yachts such as the *Drone, Swallow* and *Cupid*, built with the concave vee-shaped floor. The merits and demerits of the concave and convex shapes were hotly discussed by followers of the square chine yachts, and it is very difficult to say which is the faster type. Off the wind and sailing at their slowest speed, it has been argued that the concave vee has a tendency to suck down and cling to the water, owing to a partial vacuum forming underneath the bottom.

George Honour never wavered in his faith in the original shape of his first design. And when one studies the wonderful racing record of the various yachts which he built and sailed to victory, one may assume that even if his yachts were no better than the concave vee type, they were certainly their equal.

Eager enthusiasts of the square bilge yachts also turned their attention to improving the sail and rigging plans of new boats that had been built. The Curry brothers are notable examples of keen amateur builders who have made an exhaustive study in their endeavours to get still more speed out of new yachts. In the *Swallow* they brought out an extreme type embodying all the latest ideas in modern aerodynamics. The boat was constructed as lightly as it was possible to do without sacrificing the strength necessary to hold the hull together, her bottom planking being only 6.30 mm in thickness. She carried a tall mast 10.5 m high, and the luff rope of her Bermudian mainsail slid up inside the hollow stick, there being no track or sail clips to disturb the air flow across the sail. Weight and windage were cut to a minimum wherever possible, and on completion great interest centred round the new boat. But her subsequent racing performance was disappointing, and not until her rig was changed to the orthodox gaff sail did she begin to show her paces, eventually proving to be a very fast little craft.

George Honour, the father of square bilge yachts in New Zealand, died in 1941. With his passing the popularity of these pretty, seaworthy and easy-to-construct boats began to wane, and of the many hundreds built since the *Sasanof* was launched 60 years ago perhaps only 10 still sail the sparkling waters of the Waitemata.

10.

The small-class racers

NEW ZEALAND YACHTING has always been characterised by the large number of different classes of small centreboard yachts. In most instances these various classes owe their existence to the efforts of a single individual who designed a yacht, in many cases for his own use, to be sailed in a particular environment. A good example of this circumstance was the design of the famous but ill-fated Z-class, which became known as the Takapuna class throughout New Zealand. This 3.8 m yacht, which raced each year for the coveted Cornwell Cup, was designed by R. B. Brown of Northcote, Auckland, to sail on the tidal estuaries of Ngataringa and Shoal Bays. It proved so well suited to this type of sailing that it quickly found favour in other tidal mudflat areas such as Tauranga, Manukau and the Sumner Estuary near Christchurch.

Among other classes also developed were the Idle Along, designed for the boisterous conditions on Wellington Harbour by Alf Harvey, and the 2.1 m P-class, developed in Tauranga by Mr M. H. A. Highet.

All these classes, including the 4.3 m T and Y-classes, the 3.6 m Silver Fern (designed by the late Arch Logan), the Wakatere Scow and the Frostbite (designed by Jack Brooke) and the famous but now extinct 4.3 m overall X-class, were designed in the 20-year period between the world wars, reaching their peak of popularity in the decade after World War II.

Two factors in the 1950s combined to kill these classes and replace them with a totally different kind of small racing yacht. The first and greatest influence was the introduction of marine plywood. Although plywood had been available in New Zealand since 1938, it was not until a true marine grade plywood with totally waterproof glue came available to boatbuilders in 1953 that its effect became apparent. And what an effect it was! Overnight the traditional kauri-planked, copper-fastened, immensely strong but extremely heavy small yacht, was re-

placed by light, glued but equally strong plywood craft. New designs and designers sprang up overnight, and the home handyman boatbuilding boom began. It continues unabated today.

Many of the traditional classes were doomed, but the class administrators could not or would not see it. Economy had a big role in this dramatic upheaval, and the first class to suffer was the pretty little Silver Fern class. Other classes such as the T, Y and S (4.9 m) quickly followed, while others such as the Z, Idle Along and X classes tried to compete by allowing plywood construction. But the rule change was left too late, and these grand little boats also suffered the same fate.

The second factor, which coincided with the introduction of marine plywood, was New Zealand's entry into international yachting in 1956. In that year we first competed in the Olympic Games at Melbourne, Peter Mander and Jack Cropp winning the gold medal in the Sharpie class. New Zealand yachtsmen had tasted international success — and they liked it. A rush to international classes such as the Finn and Flying Dutchman started, at the expense of traditional indigenous designs. Local talented young designers, such as Wellington's John Spencer, produced ultra-fast plywood yachts like the Cherub and Javelin classes, which spread overseas to Australia and England. These fast-planing hulls, sailed with small crews, utilised modern developments of synthetic sail cloth, alloy spars and stainless steel rigging.

But let us go back to review the whole development of small class yachts in New Zealand.

Just over 50 years ago Mr W. A. Wilkinson, then a prominent yachtsman and administrator, suggested to Charles Bailey Junior's son Gladwyn that he should design a small-class racing yacht of 4.3 m which would be suitable for the younger generation of yachtsmen.

Glad Bailey set to work and drew out the lines of the *Desert Gold*. He placed the lines before his father and asked him for his opinion. Charles Junior made one or two suggestions and finally passed the design with the remark, "That should make a good one-design class; she should be quite alright for a start, so do not worry too much over her." The *Desert Gold* was accordingly built, and immediately created a good impression in the hands of her owners, Frank Cloke and Joe Patrick. But nobody dreamed that the boats would eventually become famous in the annals of New Zealand yachting. Yet such

proved to be the case, for two very distinguished names became directly linked with the yachts.

During Lord Jellicoe's term as Governor General of New Zealand from 1920 to 1924 he became interested in yacht racing in Auckland. Not favouring the handicapping system then ruling among the bigger yachts, he asked if there

The famous *Iron Duke*, built by Charles Bailey Junior for the Governor-General of New Zealand, Earl Jellicoe, in 1920. Here, sailed by Jellicoe, she finishes a race off Devonport Wharf in 1922. *Iron Duke* is today fully restored by the Historical Boat Society, and is on display in the Auckland Museum.

was a class which was not handicapped. Informed that there was a small-class racer just commencing, he immediately decided on one for himself. As a birthday present from Lady Jellicoe, an order was placed with the Bailey firm for a new boat of 4.3 m on the same lines as the *Desert Gold*. When the boat was almost completed His Excellency was asked to name the craft. From Wellington came the request to christen her *Betty* after Her Excellency. After informing him that there was already a boat of that name, Charles Bailey Junior received another telegram: "Name her *Iron Duke*", after the admiral's famous old flagship, which fought at the Battle of Jutland.

With such distinguished patronage, it was small wonder that the class flourished and promptly became known as the Jellicoe class. In 1921 the *Iron Duke*, with the Governor-General on board, represented Auckland in the first contest for the now-famous Sanders Cup. She was sailed in the first race by Glad Bailey, and was beaten by the *Heather*. In the succeeding races Lord Jellicoe sailed the *Iron Duke* himself and won two races, only to be beaten by the Otago representative in the finish.

The following year the contest took place in Wellington, Auckland being represented by the *Desert Gold* and Wellington by the *Iron Duke*, which had been taken south by Lord Jellicoe. *Desert Gold* was victorious and brought the cup back to Auckland.

A year later the *Rona*, built for Mr A. Gifford, was launched from Bailey's yard, and after a number of trials was chosen as the Auckland representative. Her victories were so decisive that it was decided at a meeting of the various delegates to build all future boats on the *Rona's* lines. Moulds of the *Rona* were carefully made and supplied to all intending builders of Jellicoe-class yachts. However the measurements were not always strictly adhered to, and the early history of these boats is notable for a good deal of dissension amongst those directly interested in the class. Eventually, however, a better understanding prevailed, and it was resolved to conform to the *Rona's* lines in general but to allow some slight latitude in the various hull measurements, resulting in a restricted class racer. The sail areas, however, were to be strictly limited to a certain size.

Following the *Rona* came the *Queen March*, built by the Baileys for Mr Elliott Davis. She was chosen to represent Auckland that year, but was defeated by the Dunedin representative sailed by veteran skipper Jack Wiseman.

Mr Frank Cloke, the original owner of the *Desert Gold*, now placed an order with the Baileys for another boat; the beautiful little *Avalon* was now built, creating great admiration amongst the followers of this class. The *Murihiku II*, built for a Mr Moffit of Stewart Island by the Bailey firm, was a fine boat but did not meet with great success. These six boats became the predecessors of what came to be called the Jellicoe class and laid the foundation for the development of this class. For 40 years Jellicoe craft were to be found in every sailing area throughout New Zealand.

Many other builders throughout New Zealand now contributed some fine little vessels. Boats such as *Iona*, *Betty*, *Eileen*, *Avenger*, *Irene*, *Lavina*, *Kitty* and *Huia* all won the coveted Sanders Cup Trophy.

Although the *Iron Duke* was not highly successful in Sanders Cup races, she won many prizes in other yacht club fixtures before being taken to Wellington. Under the ownership of Lord Jellicoe she was sailed in most of her races by Glad Bailey, who was the proud possessor of many trophies presented to him by the Governor General each time he won a race in the admiral's yacht.

Many little human stories are told of the famous man who liked to seek his pleasures in the little blue-hulled *Iron Duke*. To those yachtsmen amongst whom he mixed he was familiarly known as "Jellie" and he used to converse easily with all with whom he came in contact.

When the news of this great man's death was received in Auckland on 21 November 1935 yacht club flags were hauled to half-mast and yachtsmen throughout New Zealand expressed their profound sorrow at the loss of one whom they had come to like so well. The name of Lieutenant-Commander Sanders V.C. is also revered in New Zealand yachting circles, for it is after this great naval hero that the Sanders Cup is named as a perpetual memorial.

The Sanders Cup came to be regarded as the blue riband of New Zealand yachting. Each year a series of trial races was held by the yachtsmen of various ports throughout New Zealand, the winning boats becoming eligible to race for the famous cup. The annual contest was sailed at the port of the defending province, or at some other port the defending province agreed upon.

The contest was decided each year by holding a series of races until one boat won three races. The beautiful Sanders Cup trophy was presented by Walker and Hall, manufacturing jewellers, through the efforts of their manager at the time, Mr John Hislop, who was very interested in the Rona-Jellicoe class.

Lieutenant-Commander Sanders was probably the most famous of the band of New Zealand yachtsmen who served with such distinction during the Great War. He went to sea as a steward at the age of 17 and in 1906 signed on the Government steamer *Hinemoa* as an ordinary seaman. Later he joined the Craig Line of sailing ships to gain experience in sail. He then went back into steam, and at the age of 27 passed his exams for extra master. During World War I he was appointed Sub-Lieutenant R.N.R. in 1916 and later joined H.M.S. *Sabina* as second in command. Volunteering for service in Q-ships, he was given command of the small tops'l schooner *Prize*. In a little over a year he had been promoted from sub-lieutenant to lieutenant-commander, one of the most remarkable cases of rapid promotion in the history of the navy. Within a few months he had won the Victoria Cross and the Distinguished Service Order, the latter award being made after his death in action.

Besides the annual contest for the Sanders Cup, X-class yachts were engaged in racing throughout the summer season in most of New Zealand's major yachting centres. Canterbury was probably the stronghold of these little vessels — local conditions seem most suited to this particular type of yacht.

It was therefore fitting that Canterbury yachtsmen were the last to win the Sanders Cup in 1966. In that year it was decided to phase out the X-class to meet the competition from newer, faster and cheaper yachts such as the Spencer-designed Javelin (4.27 m). It was appropriate that rather than be forgotten, the Sanders Cup was transferred to this new class for annual competition. The historic *Iron Duke* is now preserved for all time in the Auckland War Memorial Museum, having been restored by members of the Historical Boat Society in 1972.

Next to the X-class in importance and seniority in terms of inter-port yacht racing, was the Z-class — yachts in this class are often referred to as the Cornwell Cup boats. They owed their existence to a small band of Takapuna yachtsmen who planned the first boat with much the same idea in their minds as did George Honour when he built the first of the 4.3 m square bilge boats — namely, low initial cost and ease of construction, with an ever-watchful eye on speed and performance under Auckland harbour weather conditions. The yachts were originally designed for the Takapuna Boating Club, but their popularity from the outset led to the type becoming quickly adopted by many other yacht clubs throughout New Zealand.

The first boat was built in 1922 by Bob Brown of Northcote, Auckland, after the committee had approved of his design. She measured 3.8 m overall, with a 1.5 m beam, and she was constructed on the square chine vee-bottom principle. The whole of her working sail area was carried in a gunter mainsail, hoisted on a stout mast stepped well forward, there being no bowsprit or headsail. In spite of this simple rig, she attained very fast speeds with the aid of a mast-head spinnaker.

Other boats quickly followed this first craft, and from small beginnings the Takapuna one-design Z-class rapidly expanded. They formed one of the largest racing classes in Auckland among the smaller yachts, no fewer than 77 of these popular little boats being entered for Anniversary Day in 1950. With watertight bulkheads fore and aft and a minimum of gear to handle, the younger generation of New Zealand yachtsmen who sailed the Z-class boats became noted for their skill in taking the craft out in really hard breezes. In the event of a capsize, they would quickly right the boat, bail out and sail away.

Apart from the usual yacht club races, the Z-class yachts engage each year in a most important event known as the Cornwell Cup contest.

The Cornwell Cup contest differs slightly from the Sanders Cup races in that it is an inter-port contest and not an inter-provincial one. Any town with recognized yacht racing is deemed to be a port — hence the inland town of Hamilton participates in Cornwell Cup matches. There are two other differences. One is that the crews comprise only two members, who must be under the age of 19 years on the first day of January in the year of the contest. The other is that the crews need not take their own boats to the scene of the contest; they may use boats of the Z-class belonging to the port, drawing for boats each time a race is held. The rules state that the boats are to be drawn for twenty-four hours prior to the first race, and that no crew may draw the same boat twice until all boats in the contest have been used by any one crew. Each crew must use its own mainsail and spinnaker throughout the races; the sails to be of strictly limited specifications and to be of New Zealand manufacture. The contest has always

been decided by sailing a series of races until one crew wins three races.

Behind the history of the Cornwell Cup contest lies the life and death story of John Travers Cornwell, Boy First Class, R.N., whose devotion to duty has gone down in history. When the Great War broke out Jack Cornwell entered the Royal Navy, and after a period of training was

A very early photograph of Bob Brown's famous Z-class yachts. Here they are rigged with their original gunter.

The Z-class, sail trainer for thousands of New Zealand yachtsmen.

fire, with just his own brave heart and God's help to support him."

John Travers Cornwell, naval hero, died two days later in Grimsby Hospital, England. He was posthumously awarded the Victoria Cross, and later nearly $40,000 was subscribed to a national memorial fund. A painting of the boy standing beside his gun with Admiral Earl Beatty's report of the incident once occupied a place in many schools.

New Zealand yachtsmen who participated in the then two most important yachting contests, the Sanders Cup and the Cornwell Cup, were thus reviving each summer the memories of three British heroes of World War I — Earl Jellicoe, Lieutenant-Commander Sanders and John Travers Cornwell.

A young designer in the 1930s who was to make a great impact on New Zealand yachting was Jack Brooke of Devonport. Mr Brooke was to achieve two of the greatest honours in New Zealand yachting — "New Zealand Yachtsman of the Year", in 1972, and commodore of the prestigious Royal New Zealand Yacht Squadron from 1969 to 1971. However all these honours were still ahead of the young Jack Brooke when he drew up the lines of the rather odd looking Wakatere Scow class in 1930. This yacht was designed for the Wakatere Boating Club, of which Brooke was a foundation member, to be raced off the open Narrow Neck Beach in the Rangitoto Channel, outside of Auckland Harbour.

The class was designed to meet certain criteria. First, the yachts had to be able to be carried out of the water on an open beach after racing; consequently the boats had to be of light construction. Second, the majority of the yacht club members were under the age of 21, so expense was a very big consideration. Third, seven of the members had canoe sails of 7 sqm area, so the boat was designed with a total sail area not in excess of this measurement. Fourth, the new class had to provide ease of construction for the totally unskilled amateur boatbuilder. With these conditions in view, a scow-bowed craft, having an overall length of 4.3 m, with small beam and light construction was decided upon.

Ten boats were built for use off Narrow Neck Beach, and were found very satisfactory, providing fast and keen racing. However because of the light construction, they did not prove entirely seaworthy in rough conditions. An improvement on the Wakatere Scow was

appointed to the light cruiser *Chester* with the rating of Boy First Class. Within a few months the lad of just 16 had been through the greatest naval battle in history and earned the highest honour that could be bestowed upon him — the Victoria Cross.

The *Chester* was scouting 8 km to starboard of the Third Battle Cruiser Squadron on the afternoon of 31 May 1916 as the grand fleet swept down towards Jutland. She came into action just after 5.30 p.m. when four German light cruisers and destroyers loomed up through the mist. Gamely she opened fire, but at once the German guns straddled her — the range was less than 5 km — and in a few minutes many of her guns were out of action, 35 men killed and over 40 wounded. Zigzagging to disconcert the enemy gunlayers, the *Chester* made off at full speed. Through it all Jack Cornwell, although badly wounded in the first few minutes of the action and with only two men left out of a gun crew of 10, stood quietly at his post awaiting orders.

"His gun would not bear on the enemy," said the captain of the *Chester* in a letter to the lad's mother, "and he was the only one who was in such an exposed position. But he felt he might be needed, and indeed he might have been, so he stayed there, standing and waiting under heavy

designed, again by Brooke. It became known as the Wakatere Cruiser — it was a standard vee-bottom knockabout with heavy scantlings and a regulation bow. Ten of these yachts were built, compared with over 50 of the scows; they competed with good results, particularly in heavy weather, against the Y-class.

The heavy construction meant that during the week the boats were pulled up on Narrow Neck Beach. In 1934, when Auckland suffered an unprecedented easterly gale, all but two were smashed to pieces. This damage to the fleet plus some design faults, particularly in the Wakatere Cruiser, meant no more were built, and both Wakatere types languished.

In 1938, after much deliberation on the part of a designs committee, it was decided to prepare the lines of a sailing dinghy to the following specifications: (1) capable of good performance under a small sail area; (2) no headsails, backstays or extras; (3) sturdy enough to be towed on a car trailer; (4) suitable for use with an outboard motor, or for service as a yacht's tender; (5) weight not to exceed 82 kg.

Other conditions called for a design suitable for amateur builders. Workmanship and design had to be so good that no unfavourable criticism could be raised. And with international competition in mind, the dimensions had to be the same as the standard American Frostbite dinghy class. These conditions were rigidly adhered to, and the first boat was drawn out by Brooke, Mr G. S. Miller arranging the scantling and plankings.

The centreboard trunk of a Frostbite dinghy embodies a fore and after girder, which stiffens the boat against shocks when being towed on a car trailer. The planking is of even width for appearance's sake, the garboards being narrow at the stem. This method also ensures straight-grained planks and eliminates the work of steaming, a kettle of boiling water on the forward end being all that is necessary. The mast is spliced, so that with the spars it can be stowed right inside the length of the boat when being transported. The rigging is of the simplest type possible. Amateur builders were offered every assistance, the club providing templates for standard parts, moulds and building trestles. Over 250 boats were built, nearly all by amateurs.

Frostbite-class dinghies have raced in all parts of the North Island. Transported by car, they have sailed on Lakes Rotorua, Rotoiti, Oka-

A close-up of a Frostbite yacht, here sailed by Neil Coleman and his son, shows the simple but efficient rig of these popular little yachts.

taina, Taupo, Hamilton and Waikaremoana. They have also been raced in Tauranga, Manukau, Kawhia, Opotiki and many other harbours in the North Island.

Because of the multi-purpose use of the Frostbite, the class has survived to the present day. Indeed, close racing still takes place every summer weekend in front of the Wakatere clubhouse at Narrow Neck Beach. The club has now introduced a fibreglass Frostbite, the mould being taken off the wooden hull. Strict specifications regarding weight are enforced, so that the old wooden boats are still competitive with those built by the new construction method.

This modern development has worked well with the 6.70 m mullet boats, and appears to be the answer when it comes to blending the old traditional construction methods, with modern developments. The older boat is not superseded, and therefore doesn't lose its value.

In 1934 Alf Harvey of Wellington realised that virtually all the centreboard yachts then sailing in New Zealand had been designed by Auckland designers for the conditions experienced on the Waitemata Harbour and Hauraki Gulf. Wellington Harbour is renowned for strong winds and associated rough seas, and many of the Auckland designs were not suited to these more robust conditions. After a series of experiments Mr Harvey developed a design which not only handled rough water but also provided competitive sailing.

His design measured 3.8 m overall and 1.8 m in beam, and was based on the square chine principal — with a good rise in the floor forward of amidships, flattening out to a broad tuck stern. The sail plan was orthodox, with a mainsail and jib totalling 12 sq m, the mainsail measuring 8.3 sq m. A spinnaker was carried for reaching and running. Attractive features of the design were watertight compartments fore and aft, which had sufficient buoyancy to allow a capsized craft to be righted and bailed out, simplicity of construction for the amateur builder and associated low cost of building. The original plan called for a gunter rig, similar to the Z-class of the time, but this was later modified to a Bermudian rig when it was found that the yachts performed better with a one-piece mast.

Alf Harvey built the prototype and called her *Idle Along*, and she attracted much great interest (not only to Wellington yachtsmen). In February 1935 the plans were submitted to the

The ever-popular Frostbites, designed by Jack Brooke in 1938, race in the Rangitoto Channel.

A fine example of Alf Harvey's Idle Along class sailing in a light breeze. These yachts normally carried two or three-man crews.

71

Wellington Provincial Yacht and Motorboat Association for approval for inter-provincial competition. In the 1935-36 season the inaugural inter-provincial competition was held on Wellington Harbour. The first winner of the Moffatt Cup, which was presented by Wellington yachtsmen in the memory of Jack Moffatt, who had been an ardent worker for yachting in Wellington, was won by a crew from Tauranga. Fittingly they were sailing Alf Harvey's original *Idle Along*, which they had borrowed for the series.

The Idle Along class thrived in the late 1940s and 1950s, but in common with other classes such as the Z and X, the change to plywood construction was left too late. The class slowly declined and finally died in the late 1960s. It was a great pity, because the design was far more wholesome than many of today's racing machines.

Another Wellington yachtsman, Harry Highet, designed the smallest competitive class in

A fine picture in the early morning sun. P-class yachts being rigged on Takapuna beach.

New Zealand and perhaps the world. The famous P-class, only 2.1 m long, has blooded and trained more New Zealand yachtsmen than all the other classes combined. This tiny yacht, which is built on the chine principle, and has a beam of 1.07 m, originally had a gunter rig, but this was changed in 1956 to the Bermuda rig. About this time far-seeing class administrators also allowed plywood construction. As a result the class thrived. Whereas other classes have died, the P-class is today stronger than ever, racing each year for the coveted Tanner and Tauranga cups.

Indeed the P-class is also known as the Tauranga class, because Mr Highet moved there from Wellington soon after designing the yacht; the first yachts from this design sailed on the Tauranga Harbour. The first inter-provincial championship was sailed in January 1940, in conjunction with the Wellington Centennial Regatta, and it was at this time that the rules were laid down for competition. They still apply today. The principle condition was that skippers of these little boats must be under 16 years of age at the time of the championship.

Many thousands of New Zealand yachtsmen, including several Olympic and offshore champion skippers, learnt to sail in P-class yachts, and it was therefore fitting that Mr Highet should be the inaugural winner of the prestigious "Yachtsman of the Year" trophy presented by the then Governor-General, Bernard Fergusson, in 1963. Because of their age restrictions the P-class and Z-class proved ideal training craft for young New Zealand yachtsmen, who then moved onto larger craft having learnt basic seamanship and yacht handling.

A common criticism of today's small-class racers is that there are too many classes, thereby diluting the hot competition which brings out the best in competing skippers and crews racing against each other in the same class. A check through the 1976 Auckland Anniversary Regatta programme shows that there were a total of 14 classes under 4.3 m racing on the day, with a total of 57 entries in the biggest class (the ever-popular P-class). This must be compared with the 1950 regatta, when there were only the P-class and Z-class under 3.6 m with a massive entry of 89 in the P-class. The Z-class entries

OK class dinghies being rigged on Takapuna Beach, Auckland. This monotype yacht, designed by Swede Knud Olsen, enjoys worldwide popularity because of its strict one-design regulations, which ensure competitive sailing.

Harry Highet's famous little sail-training craft sail on the Browns Bay School swimming pool during a class publicity stunt. P.98 *Hakaokoa* and P.571 *Tich* take young passengers for a spin.

were so numerous that the class had to be split into two divisions, Takapuna and Pupuke, to accommodate the entries (which collectively totalled 101 yachts).

In Auckland 40 years ago there were two classes at the height of their fame — the 4.8 m S-class and the 4.3 m T-class. Both were "unrestricted", in that apart from overall length and beam requirements there were no other class restrictions in terms of sail area, weight or crew size. This free and easy approach encouraged designers and builders, both professional and amateur, to experiment with hull design and rig, and accounted for the great popularity of these classes. In 1923 there were 63 S-class and 54 T-class yachts registered and by 1936 these registrations had climbed to 110 and 86 respectively. Yet by 1946 only 13 yachts were registered in the S-class and 16 in the T-class. The absence of so many young yachtsmen overseas on war service did of course account for much of this trend. The boats were laid up at the back of sections and other areas, and just rotted away. Today not one S or T-class yacht is still sailing. The classes are just a memory.

The War aside, it is rather difficult to account for their rapid decline, for in each class there were to be found many splendid little yachts, well designed and soundly constructed. It can only be assumed that it was not due to any design defect, but rather that the yachting population was simply becoming more distributed among many small-class racers.

Prior to 1955 (which can be termed the "before plywood" era) there were a total of 13 classes of racing yachts, 5.5 m and under, all of which flourished and eventually declined. Following the introduction of plywood in the early 1950s (and, in the present decade, moulded fibreglass) a further 22 classes have appeared in New Zealand yachting. The majority are local designs, but the modern trend is toward the factory-produced, franchise-sold, fibreglass yachts of North American design — such as the Laser. It is interesting to note that even the Cherub, the first of the classes designed for plywood construction back in 1954 (of which there have been nearly 2000 built), could only raise a racing fleet of 11 boats in the 1976 Anniversary Regatta. It would appear that this class is now on the decline.

However there is one class of yacht still racing and capable of arousing the interest of even non-yachtsmen, and that is the spectacular, un-

Perhaps the most modern small boat class in New Zealand. A Wind Rush Surfcat stretches its sails off Takapuna Beach.

restricted, famous 5.5 m (18 ft) V-class. It seems hard to believe that these "pure" racing machines, virtually all of them sponsored by commercial concerns, have a history which dates back half a century — to 1922, when George Honour designed and build Wizard. The class was adopted by the Royal Akarana Yacht Club (in those days just the plain Akarana Yacht Club) and by 1923 11 boats were racing. From 19 starts, Wizard won 11 first, five seconds and three third prizes.

Another fast boat racing at that time in the V-class was the Secret, a 5.5 m mullet boat designed by Arch Logan and built by Ben Mayall in 1922. The Secret has the distinction of being

The late Clive Roberts as many remember him, sailing to the limit in a Finn class yacht. Roberts was also prominent in the OK class, winning the World Championship in 1973 in England.

the first yacht to be constructed on the raised-deck principle, and she was also one of the first boats in New Zealand to carry the Marconi rig.

In 1923 a number of new yachts made their appearance, among them being the Logan-designed *Surprise* (which was built by Mayall and Bill Couldrey), *Wildwave*, *Millicent* and *Leveret*. They were all square bilge yachts and fast sailers, the *Surprise* being an outstanding example of the few boats of this type designed by the master builder Arch Logan. Along with *Secret*, *Surprise* was the first square bilge boat to carry the Marconi rig, which is really the predecessor of our present-day lofty Bermudian sails.

From such small beginnings the number of V-class yachts now steadily increased in the following years, for numerous amateur builders began to invade the V-class field. Among these early amateurs, the name of A. (Trott) Willetts stands out prominently.

Having constructed many 4.3 m square bilge boats, of which the *Cupid*, built in 1922, was the

The E-class yacht *La Mouette*, a gulf cruiser designed by Colin Wild, reaches across Auckland harbour. This class of yacht has proved ideally suited to the conditions around the northern coast of the North Island.

forerunner, "Trott" Willetts turned his attention to the V-class. His first boat, the *Drone* — which he designed in 1925 for Gordon Curry who built her — certainly made an impression. For some seasons she was an outstanding yacht on the Waitemata, finally going to the Manukau Harbour, where she continued to race successfully for some years. The following year he designed and supervised the building of the *Belle* for Mr T. Tait. Two other prominent boats at this time were the *Magic* and the *Mystic*, both designed and built by George Honour.

It was at this stage that the fleet, composed mostly of square bilge craft carrying the gaff rig, began to assume some importance. Racing was becoming keener each season, and besides sailing harbour courses the V-class yachts were participating in cruising races (for most of the early boats were decked in and fitted out for this purpose). For many years they raced annually to the harbour of Te Kouma on the Coromandel Peninsula, a distance of 500-odd km. This race, which was sailed at night, was always a most popular fixture. Then during a race in heavy weather 30 years ago, two of the yachts capsized in the gulf, fortunately without loss of life. After this mishap, the racing officials wisely decided that no more unballasted boats would be allowed to enter this event.

The year 1932 saw the beginning of an unprecedented building boom in the V-class. Following quickly, one after the other, came such boats as Ralph Goodwin's *Marianne* and *Manutere*, and Willett's *Martha S* in 1932, *Jewell* in 1934, *Riptide* in 1935 and *Irena* in 1936. The *Martha S*, the *Riptide* (built for Mr B. Schmidt, who today owns *Innismara*) and *Irena* (for Mr E. Carr) are fine examples of this amateur builder's work. Other fast models built about this time include Billy Rogers's *Arline* and *Atalanta*, also a long list of yachts designed and built by Arnold ("Bill") Couldrey.

By 1935 the V-class had grown tremendously and the racing was so keen that builders were in constant demand, designing and constructing new craft for V-class racing enthusiasts. This rapid building programme naturally brought the standard of the V-class to a very high pitch.

There is no doubt that Couldrey himself contributed greatly in this respect, for commencing with the *Hawk* and the *Shamrock* in 1935, he quickly followed these boats up by building such notable craft as *Limerick*, *Mamaru*, *Jeanette*, *Athena* and *Marie Dawn*.

V-class cruising "eighteens" and the smaller S-class racing in St. Marys Bay, Auckland harbour, in 1928. Leading is *Champagne* (V.6) from *Sun* (V.7), with *Secret* (V.3), *Ben Bolt* (S.48) and *Spindrift* following. Note that *Sun's* forestay has hit *Champagne's* boom.

A further photograph of the *Sun*, here leaving Islington Bay on Rangitoto Island in 1931.

In later years another amateur designer and builder, Jack Brooke, has added to the ranks of the V-class. His designs such as *Kiwi*, *Arahi* (built by Colin Wild) and *Kiatere* have all set the pace on various occasions.

Many changes have come about since the formation of the V-class. The very earliest yachts were widely divergent types of square bilge craft, some of light displacement, others heavy and somewhat cumbersome. With no restrictions other than on overall length, amateur designers and builders had a free hand.

By 1940 the square bilge boats were definitely on the wane. They had served a most useful purpose in establishing the V-class, but they were now being replaced by round-bilge and faster craft. It was also obvious that the majority of these yachts being built were now being built for racing, with no thought of being used for cruising. It was a far cry from the original concept of a cruising boat which also took part in races.

Of the 300 or so square bilge craft which George Honour designed and built, only a very few now remain.

Perhaps the best example of this type of yacht left sailing is the *Sun*, formerly called the *Millicent*. As we have seen, she was designed by George Honour and launched in November 1922. Honour also built her to the frame stage in conjunction with the *Wizard*. The *Millicent* was

77

then bought by a Ponsonby yachtsman who finished her off. She was renamed *Sun* in 1927, when she was sponsored by the now defunct *Auckland Sun* newspaper. This appears to be the earliest instance of sponsorship in New Zealand yachting history; it predated this now common practice by 40 years. The *Sun* is now fully restored and still sails the waters of the Waitemata Harbour (with the author at the helm).

The value of international competition is clearly shown in the survival of the "eighteens" as they are now affectionately called. That this class is still flourishing when others are long dead is due primarily to the G. G. Giltinan trophy, which is an inter-dominion contest between New Zealand and Australia (although entries have been received from Fiji — where one series was actually sailed).

"Eighteens" (that is, 5.5 m) had been sailed on Sydney Harbour for many years and had in fact been backed like racehorses by bookies who followed the racing fleets with the punters in chartered harbour ferries. These Australian yachts were real "man-killers", carrying enormous crews of up to 12 men. When reaching or running set ringtails and watersails, as well as spinnakers, they would be using a total sail area of well over 90 sq m.

Controversy raged for years over whether the Auckland "eighteens" could beat the Sydney flyers, and in 1938 four Auckland craft — *Riptide*, *Vaalele*, *Irena* and *Manene* — were shipped to Australia and raced against the world famous Sydney yachts. In mostly light winds the Auckland team was soundly beaten, and the long-debated question as to whether or not these great sail-carrying Australian flyers were as fast as everyone had been led to believe seemed to be settled once and for all.

In February 1939, in a spirit of goodwill and sportsmanship, the Australians returned our visit, bringing over three of their yachts — *Malvina*, *St. George*, and the new champion and holder of the world title, the famous *Taree*. Any ideas that may have been expressed by followers of the sport that Australia was going to have a runaway victory were quickly dispelled. Racing

St. George, one of the three Australian 18-footers to visit Auckland in 1939. She is to windward of *Jeanette*.

The famous Australian 18-footer *Taree* reaching in a fresh breeze on Sydney Harbour. Note the eight-man crew necessary to control these powerful sail carriers. *Taree* was at this time the world champion.

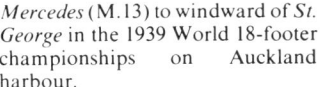

Mercedes (M.13) to windward of *St. George* in the 1939 World 18-footer championships on Auckland harbour.

in hard as well as light breezes, the Auckland team showed their paces in a most remarkable manner, winning the first two heats and eventually gaining the coveted title, which was won by Chamberlain and Goodfellow's M-class yacht *Manu*. The V-class boat *Jeanette*, which was splendidly sailed throughout the contest by Jim Faire, and incidentally met with some really hard luck, gained second place on points.

From an observer's point of view, the pace of the Australian yachts in light breezes was phenomenal, but we must remember the enormous sails carried by the Sydney craft. On the other hand, in the hard two-reef breeze of the first heat, it was obvious almost from the commencement of the race that the Auckland yachts were footing faster and sailing closer on the wind. Rounding the weather mark off Watchman Island in the first heat shortly after the start, the Aucklander *Jeanette* was planing off the wind at terrific speed. One of the Australian yachts some distance astern seemed to be wallowing along with no life in her hull.

This lifelessness was attributable to two factors. In the first instance, the hard breeze in the early afternoon caused the Australian skippers to rig their yachts with the smallest of the three suits of racing sails which go with their craft. When the wind became lighter just after the start, the visiting yachts found themselves under-canvassed — but nothing could be done to remedy this unfortunate state of affairs. On the other hand Auckland craft, carrying their usual racing sails, were able to reef or shake out at will, right up to within a few minutes of the starting gun.

The other reason for this sluggishness was the weight of a heavy crew sinking down a hull lacking natural buoyancy. Fashioned on the lines of a type long since extinct among wholesome racing yachts, the Sydney craft were built up from a V-shaped midship section reminiscent of the "pegtop"-sectioned craft of years ago. Yachtsmen who have studied both this shape and the records of boats designed on these lines know that there is certainly speed in this hull form — but also that this type of yacht lacks that vital necessity for heavy windward work which we call "power", unless a big sail area is carried.

Over the nearly 40 years since the very first G. G. Giltinan trophy race was sailed, the "eighteens" on both sides of the Tasman have changed dramatically. Gone are the heavy, beamy, powerful hulls driven by massive sail areas and controlled by large crews. In their place have developed ultra-light, easily driven hulls built of plywood, glass or even foam, with high aspect ratio rigs and single overlapping headsails. The crew is of three or maybe four men, all on trapezes. These modern yachts sail as fast if not faster than their predecessors, particularly on the wind, but reaching or running they would be left by the massive sail carriers, particularly in fresh conditions.

This transition did not come overnight. It developed gradually through the era of the famous skimmers, such as *Komutu* and *Tarua*, designed and built by Jack Logan in the 1950s, to the orthodox straight-stemmers such as *Result* and *Daniel Boone* in the early 1960s, then later in that decade to the Peter Mander-inspired *Intrigue*. The 1970s saw the start of sponsorship and yachts designed by budding geniuses like Bruce Farr and the late Frank Blackburn (tragically killed at an early age in a road accident). A succession of *Travelodges* and other yachts like *Captain Morgan*, *Cool Leopard* and *Ah Bisto* have continued the current trend to the light easily driven "eighteen" with a moderate sail area.

New Zealand small-class yachting is in a state of flux in the mid 1970s. It is obvious that 20-year-old designs such as the Cherub and the Arrow are on the way out like the Silver Fern, X-class and Idle Alongs they replaced. The question is what will replace the Cherubs, Arrows, Javelins and Q-class. It appears that the old P-class will be with us forever as a child's trainer, but the trend to international classes (the Finns, OK Dinghy, and Flying Dutchmen) will continue — to the detriment of local designers and to New Zealand yachting in general. Since the sport started 120 years ago, it has always been characterised by yachts designed for specific conditions indigenous to this country. What is suited to European or North American lakes or seaways is not necessarily best suited to the waters of the Waitemata Harbour, Port Nicholson or Lyttelton Harbour.

Right: A modern "eighteen". The Bruce Farr-designed *Captain Morgan* really flying off Devonport with all three men on trapeze.

11.

The cruiser of today

THE YEAR 1920 ushered in the dawn of a new era in the history of New Zealand yachting. Until this time New Zealand cutter yachts could be divided, broadly speaking, into three distinct types which, for the purposes of identification, are exemplified in some of Auckland's present-day craft.

For that very early period, from 1850 and onwards for the next 30-odd years, such boats as the famous old *Jessie Logan, Maybelle, Awatea, Why-Not, Dolphin* and *Mahoe* are excellent examples. These yachts represent the early type of plumb stem, counter stern craft, of fairly heavy displacement. They were deep-sectioned boats, slack in the bilge and ballasted well down in the water.

Without exception these early yachts carried the low-cut gaff mainsail, cutter rig, long bowsprit and, in some cases, a gaff topsail. They were "wet boats", sailing at a steep angle of heel, but they were quite wholesome for they were never carried to the extremes of similar craft being built in England about this period. Owing to the rating rule, which taxed beam heavily, English cutters were becoming so deep and narrow that they were often referred to as "planks on edge", or "lead mines". They were not altogether unknown in this country; the one-time Wellington cutter *Isca* was a typical "plank on edge".

That these plumb-stemmed boats were fast is proved by an examination of the racing record of the little Logan cutter *Maybelle*, for up to seven years ago this veteran craft could still show her stern to many of her modern sisters in the class in which she raced.

From about 1885 until 1900 the straight-stemmers had to make way for a second and new type of vessel. These boats may be called the "*Gloriana*-type". They were still fairly narrow for their length and carried the low-cut gaff rig and counter stern. Like the straight-stemmers, they were very "wet" boats. the main change in this second type was, of course, the new clipper bow and rounded forefoot.

Following the clipper-bowed type came the third type, the racing cutters of today, lighter in displacement, harder sectioned on the bilge, and possessing the "spoon" bow.

During the next 20 years these three distinct types — straight-stem, clipper-stem and spoon — were to be seen racing and cruising in all the main ports of New Zealand, the former two gradually losing ground and the latter gaining in popularity each year.

In the year 1921 still another type of cutter made its appearance on the Waitemata Harbour, and following in its wake came the cruiser of today. One of the first yachts of this type was the *Eunice*, designed by one Mr Jamieson and built by Charles Bailey Junior. She measured 7.3 m overall, 2.4 m in beam and 1.4 m in draught. Unlike the majority of small cutters of that period, this new craft had very short overhangs, was wider in the beam and possessed a great deal more room. In the same year a much larger yacht of the same type named the *Restless* was built; today she is well-known throughout New Zealand waters.

Early in the history of the cruiser class there were two amateur designers and builders whose names stood out prominently, for Mr B. S. Woollacott of Stanley Bay and the Tercel brothers of Ponsonby invaded the cruiser field in its infancy. Today both names are connected with a number of fine vessels of various sizes which were built by these amateurs during the years since the class first started.

The first yacht built by the Tercel brothers was the *Naiad*, a vee-bottom chine boat built from the same design as Thomas Fleming Day's famous yawl, *Seabird*, which crossed the Atlantic many years ago. She was built to exactly the same specifications as the American yacht, with the exception that she was ballasted with lead on her keel. She was iron-fastened throughout, was very strongly built and proved to be fast and

The old champion *Maybelle*, owned by Babs Webster for nearly 50 years. She was built in 1893 by the Logan brothers as a fishing boat, a calling she followed for many years.

able. On one occasion she won the ocean race to Tauranga, a distance of 194 km.

Following the *Naiad* came the *Restless*, a particularly fine type of short-ended cutter. As we have noted, this yacht might be said to be the forerunner of modern ocean-going cruisers, for very early in her career she proved her weatherly qualities by sailing to Wellington, where she was owned for many years. Launched in 1921, the *Restless* measures 12.2 m overall, 10.3 on the waterline, 4.1 m in beam and 1.7 m draught. She is a two-skin diagonal vessel, copper-fastened throughout, and carries 5.5 tonnes of lead on her keel. Originally gaff cutter rigged, she was later changed to jib-headed yawl and spent many years in Wellington waters. in 1953 her owner, Mr McLean, sailed her back to Auckland with the aid of a small crew, and she eventually changed hands again. *Restless* was later re-rigged as a Bermudian ketch, and still sails the waters of the Waitemata Harbour.

The *Restless* was followed in 1922 by Woollacott's first design the *Rover*, which was built on the vee-bottom chine principle. She measures 7.6 m overall, by 2.7 m beam, and is iron-fastened throughout. The yacht has a single skin of kauri planking, fastened to sawn frames of Australian jarrah. Her keel stem and stern-post are of the same wood. She sails under a Bermudian sloop rig of a total area of 46 sq m. Just prior to World War II the *Rover* was sold to a Wellington yachtsman.

In the same year that the *Rover* was built, Colin Wild constructed for himself the cruiser *Delville*, measuring 8.8 m overall, 6.8 m on the waterline, 2.4 m in beam and 1.2 m draught. She is a single-skin vessel, and carries a Bermudian sloop rig of 50 sq m, her displacement being 3.5 tonnes. Some years after she was built, the *Delville* was lengthened by about 1.2 m; she was owned for many years by Mr K. Draffin, who raced her very successfully under the name of *Kotuku*.

Following the *Delville*, Mr R. B. Brown of Northcote built in 1923 the *Reverie* for Dr Chesson of Auckland. This fine little craft was built from a design by the late Albert Strange of England, and measured 8.3 m overall, 2.3 m in beam and 1.3 m draught. She was rigged as a Bermudian sloop, having an area of 41 sq m. On her keel outside she carried 1520 kg of iron ballast. Nothing in the way of time, workmanship or material was spared this yacht, and for many years Dr and Mrs Chesson roamed the Hauraki Gulf in this fine little single-hander, eventually sailing her to their new home in Kerikeri, North Auckland. Some years ago Dr Chesson was advised to give up the sailing life for health reasons, and the *Reverie* made a re-appearance on the Waitemata Harbour under new ownership.

In 1924 Woollacott built what was at the time one of the smallest cruisers in New Zealand waters. This little craft, known as the *Lucy*, was built for Mr S. Melling of Auckland and measured but 4.9 m overall, by 1.8 m beam and 1 m draught. She carried half a tonne of lead ballast on her keel, and had a displacement of 1066 kg. The *Lucy* is a sweet little model, sails well and has an astonishing amount of room below decks for such a midget yacht.

We've now seen that during the years 1921-24 a variety of new small craft were built. They were the forerunners of the vast fleet of present-day cruisers afloat in the many different ports in New Zealand.

That yachtsmen did not take kindly to the new craft on their first appearance is natural, for the full worth of these short-ended vessels was not fully understood. To the majority of boat owners their looks were greatly against them. The yachts were totally different from anything to be seen afloat in New Zealand at that time, and the armchair critics passed many caustic comments. The majority of these critics had been used to sitting much closer to the water; when close-hauled on a wind, they spent much time admiring the rush of green water past the cabin windows. In their ignorance they considered that they sailed a great deal faster than these new-fangled yachts which seemed to sit bolt upright,

and never wet their decks.

Those who were wise enough to see past the short overhangs and high freeboard were satisfied that the cruiser was the birth of a great idea. Until the new cruiser appeared owners of small cutters of, say, 9 m or under were obliged to put up with many trials and discomforts while engaged in coastwise racing or cruising. Owing to lack of headroom, living conditions on board the early type of yacht were often very uncomfortable and in wet weather, cramped accommodation would often curtail what otherwise might have been a very pleasant cruise. Then again, in heavy weather, sails had to be constantly reefed or taken in, for small cutters of the early type were built mainly for racing and it is impossible to turn a racer into a successful cruiser. It is therefore not surprising that the ardent band of yachtsmen who preferred cruising to racing fastened eagerly onto this new type of yacht.

In 9 m it was found possible to have all the room, seaworthiness and solid comfort previously associated with a racing yacht of 13 to 15 m. This sounds astonishing until we remember that an average 13 m racer is only about 9 m on the waterline. Designers saw immediately that it was possible to produce a mighty fine little ship of a quite modest overall length without having to resort to enormous overhangs.

The advent of the cruiser opened up an entirely new field in the designing world. No longer were designers troubled with the question as to how many beams should go to the waterline length, for here was a craft which could have short ends, with the rudder stock housed in a slightly overhanging counter — or no counter at all, the rudder simply swinging on pintles on a transom stern. Providing due attention was paid to good wholesome lines combined with an efficient sail plan, designers were assured of turning out a good type of vessel.

It was in the cruiser class, too, that rapid progress was made in introducing and perfecting the Bermudian rig. Early in the history of this type, designers availed themselves of the opportunity of making the most use of this simple and efficient method of sail planning, which was just beginning to take the yachting world by storm.

In 1928 Woollacott brought out a new yacht called the *Vectis*, which was followed two years later by the *Medina*; both these names come from the Isle of Wight, where Woollacott had lived before migrating to New Zealand. *Vectis* measures 9.7 m overall, 7.9 m on the waterline, 2.7 m in beam and 1.5 m draught. She is a single-skin vessel, with sawn pohutukawa frames and steam-bent timbers. She carries a Bermudian cutter rig of 55 sq m and has a displacement of 9.5 tonnes. The *Vectis* is a fine type of offshore cruiser and has an exceptionally good deck layout — a short coachroof, wide side decks and long fore-deck. The *Vectis* was for many years owned by the late Alan Doull, secretary of the Royal New Zealand Yacht Squadron for a long period. The *Medina* is slightly shorter overall but longer on the waterline than *Vectis*, measuring 9.1 m, by 8.5 m by 2.7 m beam and 1.5 m draught. She was constructed in the same manner as the former boat, and rigged as a staysail schooner.

In 1935 Woollacott designed the *Rambler*. The hull was built in Percy Voss's yard, and the remainder of the construction carried out by her designer. She measures 10.6 m overall, 9.4 m on the waterline, 3 m in beam and 1.7 m draught, her displacement being 11.6 tonnes. This yacht was an excellent example of a cruiser of this period, being roomy, fast and able in a seaway.

Perhaps one of the best known, certainly one that has sailed the most blue water kilometres, is the sweetly-lined *Ghost*, which Woollacott built for himself and launched in 1939. She is a three-skin, diagonally-planked yacht measuring 8.5 m overall, 7.6 m on the waterline and 2.4 m in beam and draws 1.3 m. She is Bermudian sloop-rigged, with 40 sq m of working sails.

Ghost typifies the sound, seaworthy type of short end keeler which Bert Woollacott designed and which so many New Zealanders have amateur-built and sailed across oceans. Indeed Woollacott-designed yachts have created many precedents in New Zealand ocean racing and cruising. The first New Zealand yacht to sail around the world was the Woollacott-designed *Marco Polo*, skippered by Tony Armit. The inaugural Hobart to Auckland ocean race in 1952 was won by the Woollacott-designed and built *Ladybird* (she was skippered by Bert Woollacott's son John, and in the crew was Madge Woollacott, his daughter — a real family effort). The first Auckland to Suva ocean race in 1956 was won by another Woollacott boat, also built by Bert — the *Wanderer*, sailed by Tom Buchanan.

The *Wanderer* measures 9.4 m overall, 8.5 m at the waterline, with a 2.9 beam and a dis-placement of 9.6 tonnes. She has a most interesting history. She was launched in 1945 as Woollacott's "dream ship", in which he with his son and daughter as crew intended to sail around Cape Horn to England, his birthplace. This trip never eventuated, because Mr Woollacott fell down the *Wanderer's* open hatchway and seriously damaged his legs. The "dream ship" was sold, and Bert Woollacott never visited England.

A short bespectacled man with sparkling blue eyes, Bert Woollacott died in 1958. He left behind him very many sailing memorials to his designing skill.

Perhaps the fastest of all the yachts he designed was the *West Wind*, a most unlikely Woollacott yacht in that she had long overhangs but also the typical powerful midsection found in all his boats. The *Rambler*, owned by the Schiska brothers for over 30 years, is another fast Woollacott design. *Gloaming, Black Rose, Gesture, Ladybird, Blue Water, Clair de Lune, Horizon, Pastime, Tanganui,* the ill-fated *Tatariki, Wolf* — the list is endless — are other well-known and well performed Woollacott-designed yachts. It is interesting to note that those last eight yachts all raced in the Auckland to Suva race in 1966; they comprised 21 percent of the total fleet, a tribute to Bert Woollacott eight years after his death.

John Woollacott, Bert's only son, has carried on the family designing tradition, producing such well-known yachts as *Truant*, which Martin Foster sailed around New Zealand in 1972, and *Shimmer*, a 7.6 ketch.

Another family which has had a remarkable influence on New Zealand yachting in the area of keeler design and construction is that of the Tercel brothers of Ponsonby. As we have noted, their first yacht was the hard-chined *Naiad*, launched in 1919. The powerful *Restless* followed in 1921, followed in 1934 by the 7.9 m overall *Roxane*, a Bermudian rigged sloop. She is constructed of single-skin kauri, fastened to steam-bent timbers, and measures 2.4 m in the beam and 1.9 m in draught on her 7.9 m overall length. *Roxane* attracted public interest when in April 1937, crewed by Dick Wellington (who was later killed in World War II) Keith Dawson, and Lionel O'Brien, she sailed from Auckland for Sydney via Norfolk and Lord Howe Islands, eventually destined for Java (now of course Indonesia). At that time she made history as the smallest New Zealand vessel to carry a clearance

A study in stem profiles. Yachts of varying design and age in the Devonport Yacht Club yard in 1976.

The mighty *Ranger*, still perhaps the fastest yacht in New Zealand. She is carrying her old sail plan of staysail and yankee jib, reaching at over 10 knots during an Auckland first division race in 1958.

for an overseas port, being only 6.7 m on the waterline. *Roxane* reached Sydney after an uneventful passage and was sold to an Australian yachtsman.

The next Tercel brothers yacht was the fast and powerful *Roiaata*, launched in 1935. *Roiaata*, which became very well-known on the Auckland harbour, measured 9.7 m overall, 7.9 m on the waterline, 2.9 m in beam and 1.5 m in draught. She was of two-skin diagonal construction, and cutter-rigged. For many years *Roiaata* dominated the Royal New Zealand Yacht Squadron's old third division, until she was purchased by the Gillard brothers, who with a local crew sailed her to Sydney and places beyond.

During the 1930s the Tercels also built two other cutters, the *Revel* and *Reliance*, but it was not until 1938 that they launched the mighty *Ranger*, the best-known yacht in New Zealand. This craft of radical design (at the time of her launching) can today, 40 years later, still be called the champion yacht of New Zealand in

86

spite of many challengers, such as that in 1948 when the big cutter *Erewhon* was built by Colin Wild at Stanley Bay. Although the *Ranger* cannot be termed a cruiser (although she is used for that purpose every Christmas) it is appropriate to give details of what was to be the last yacht designed and built by the Tercel brothers.

Ranger measures a mighty 24.3 m overall, 13.7 m on the waterline and 3 m in beam, draws 2.3 m and displaces 11.6 tonnes. She is constructed of kauri on the three-skin diagonal principle, and is ballasted with 5.8 tonnes of lead on her keel. When launched she had a rectangular sectioned, hollow wooden mast, which measured 21.3 m from keel to truck. Yet her main boom was a tiny 6.7 m, and it was this very high aspect ratio rig which created the storm of controversy when she was launched. Her total working sail area of mainsail and foresail totalled only 92 sq m, this area being augmented, of course, by extras set when reaching or running. This sail area was compared by the experts with the A-class champions in 1938. The *Ariki* (1.8 m shorter overall) carried 148 sq m of sail on her gaff cutter rig, with a main boom 12.2 m long. The *Rainbow* (3 m shorter) carried 111 sq m of sail.

The experts considered *Ranger* to be too "modern". She would be a flop. Yet from her very first race *Ranger* proved a champion, and has continued to do so to this day. She has been modified over the years as modern technology has developed new materials and design advancements. The 21.3 m mast fell overboard 15 years ago and was replaced by an alloy spar 1 m shorter and of thicker section. The old three-crosstree rigging pattern was replaced by a more conventional two-tree system. The tiller steering was dispensed with and in its place a modern destroyer-type wheel fitted. The old cotton sails are now replaced by modern synthetic cloth, and only one brother is still alive to skipper her. Lou Tercel, nearly 80 years old, still sails *Ranger* to victory; his brother passed away many years ago. The *Ranger* will remain the yardstick with which to measure any new challenger for her laurels for many years, and will ensure that the name of Tercel will be remembered in New Zealand yachting.

There were many other yachtbuilders and designers who contributed greatly to the New Zealand yachting fleet in the period between the world wars and in the immediate post-war period.

Percy Voss designed and built in 1937 the ill-fated *Argo*, which was lost in the Wellington to Lyttelton race in 1951. Other well-known yachts he also designed and built were the fast cruiser *Tangaroa* (1936), the 7.6 m canoe-sterned *Quest* and the 8.5 m cutter *Escape* (1940).

Colin Wild of Stanley Bay also had a great impact on yacht design and building at that time and in fact right up to 1953 when his sheds and business were destroyed by fire. The first well-known keeler he built was as we've seen, the *Delville* in 1922. Other yachts included the *Tawhiri* (which won the 1940 centennial Wellington to Lyttelton ocean race), *Vida*, and several K-class yachts in the 1950s such as *Dolita* (for Sir Keith Park) and *Kitenui*.

However Colin Wild became very well-known for the design and construction of four yachts in particular. The first of these was the cutter *Nga Toa*, which was built for the Winstone family in 1926 and proved to be a particularly sound and fast family cruiser. The next was the *Ngataringa*, launched in 1940 for Mr Roger Philson of Stanley Point, Auckland. The *Ngataringa* was shorter than the *Nga Toa*, measuring 13.1 m overall, but she too proved a very seaworthy and powerful vessel.

The next was Wild's "dream ship", the *Tara*, which he started building in 1939 but because of

Great yachts old and new. *Ranger* carries spinnaker down the Waitemata Harbour, with the equally famous *Ariki* and *Fidelis* in the background.

This close-up shows *Ranger's* deck layout, which has not altered much since her launching in 1938. The major difference involves the steering, but the old-fashioned method of reefing the mainsail has been retained. In the background the John Spencer-designed *Scheherazade* runs past with spinnaker set.

the war was not able to complete until 1949. *Tara's* hull and construction was conventional enough, measuring 18 m overall, 11.9 m on the waterline, 3.6 m in the beam and drawing 2.3 m of water. However above the deckline *Tara* was certainly unconventional, having a bipod mast which straddled her foredeck and terminated 20.4 m above the deck. This was no new idea of Colin Wild's — he had rigged the *Delville* back in 1922 with a tripod mast. But it did not prove successful and was soon removed.

What Colin Wild tried to prove with these rigs is difficult to understand. He certainly did away with the need for standing rigging, but the two big hollow oregon spars on the *Tara* created enormous wind resistance compared with the conventional single mast. Wild cruised extensively in *Tara*; she was one of the first yachts to circumnavigate the North Island (in December 1951). He also raced her in the 1951 trans-Tasman race. On Wild's death in 1958, the *Tara* was sold to the Galbraith brothers of Takapuna, who raced and cruised her extensively. During their ownership the bipod masts were removed and replaced by a conventional mast and rigging. *Tara* was lost off the east coast of Australia in 1976.

The biggest yacht (it was really a motor sailer) built by Colin Wild was the *Windhaven* for Mr Berridge Spencer. This fine example of a powerful but seakindly hull, magnificently built and finished, marked the peak of Colin Wild's career — although he did build some very fine motor launches and small-class yachts. Bob

Wild, Colin's brother, is also a boatbuilder and designer of some repute, having his yard at Hamilton.

Another family who designed and built some sound yachts were the Lidgard brothers. Their first yacht was the *Ariel*, which was actually built in the yard of the Lane Motor Boat Co. up the Tamaki River. They moved to their own yard at St. Mary's Bay, and built such well-known short-end keelers as *Oreti*, *Corsair*, *Konini* (owned for 17 years by the late Tom Blackman who died in 1965), *Silver Cloud*, *Kiatere* (who has spent most of her life in Wellington) and *Heremoa*. The Lidgard brothers and Colin Wild both trained apprentices who were later to achieve boatbuilding and design success in their own right. The late Brin Wilson worked for the Lidgards and actually married one of their daughters, while Owen Woolley served his time with Wild.

The Lidgard family suffered a major tragedy in 1968 when three generations of the family were lost at sea somewhere off North Cape while en route to New Caledonia to salvage a Japanese

fishing trawler wrecked in that area (see chapter 13). Roy Lidgard, who lived at Smelting House Bay, Kawau Island, his son Jim and one of Roy's grandsons, together with two other crew workers, were on board the vessel (a former fuel tender for RNZAF flying boats at Suva, Fiji).

Roy Lidgard was particularly well-known among world cruising yachtsmen for the hospitality he extended to them at Kawau; many books written by these yachtsmen mention the Lidgard family with gratitude. His son Jim was also well-known, representing New Zealand in the world 18-foot (5.49 m) championships in such boats as *Beverly*, *Beverly Too*, *Waimarie* and *Petite*. Jim was running the family boat-building business at Bayswater, Auckland, where such well-known keelers as *Ariel* and *Fidelis* were designed and built.

Roy Lidgard had also designed and built the *Ranger* challenger *Defiant* at his yard then situated at Bon Accord Harbour, Kawau Island. *Defiant* measured 17.08 m overall, 13.2 m on the waterline, 2.9 m in beam and 2.3 m in draught. She had a similar rig to *Ranger* — a very high aspect ratio rig on a 20.7 m mast and a 7.3 m boom — but she proved to be no match for *Ranger* and dropped out of the racing scene very quickly.

Colin Wild's "dream ship". The yawl *Tara*, here slogging up the Waitemata Harbour. In this photograph there is no sign of her original unorthodox bipod mast. She was lost at sea off the Australian coast in 1976.

Amateur designers were also prominent at this time. We mentioned Jack Brooke in our chapter on small-class racers; he was also earning a reputation for the design of fast cruising keelers. The first he designed was the 10.3 m *Gleam*, which he states was an adaptation of an American one-design class. *Gleam* had a 7.9 m waterline, a 2 m beam and a draught of 1.3 m; she was launched in 1940. She was built by the amateur builders Bob and Jim Gibson of Devonport. Other Brooke designs followed, notably *Judith* (named after his daughter) in 1950, *Whitewings* (a part sister ship) in 1952, and his present boat, the K-class *Kiariki*, in 1965. Jack Brooke also had the honour of designing the *Spirit of Adventure* for the L. J. Fisher Trust as a sail training vessel in 1972.

Another well-known amateur designer was Bob Stewart, who early in his career was fortunate to have been trained by the late Arch Logan. The Logan influence — the powerful mid-section, graceful sheer with well-balanced ends and the fine entry and long run aft — were apparent in Bob Stewart's early designs, although his first design was a short-end keeler, the *Anita*, which was built for his father by the late Percy Voss in Auckland in 1935. *Anita* was built of kauri on the three-skin diagonal princi-

ple (again a Logan influence) and measured 8.5 m overall, 7.2 m at the waterline and 2.6 m in the beam. She was Bermudian sloop-rigged and proved a very good and sound cruiser, still afloat and well maintained today. Bob Stewart's next design was the well-known *Matutua*, which measured 12.9 m overall, 9.3 m on the waterline, 3.8 m in beam, with a draught of 1.4 m. This shallow draught was a direct result of the *Matutua* being designed for the tidal conditions of the Tauranga Harbour. She was built in Tauranga and launched in December 1947. She was built of kauri, again on the three-skin diagonal principle; her deck and coamings were constructed from teak salvaged from the old naval warship *Philomel* (after whom the naval base at Auckland is named) when she was scrapped in 1947.

However it was Bob Stewart's next design which really established his reputation as a designer of attractive yet fast and seaworthy yachts. This yacht was the sweetly lined *Helen*, which he designed for himself and which was built by Colin Wild and launched in November

The training ship *Spirit of Adventure* sails down the Waitemata Harbour on yet another sail training cruise. In the background the old ferry *Kestrel*, which plied across the harbour for 60 years, goes about her business.

1947. The design history of *Helen* is very interesting for it dates from 1946, when the Royal New Zealand Yacht Squadron established a special committee to draw up the restrictions and scantlings for a racing cruiser class suitable for the waters of the Hauraki Gulf, one which would appeal to members returning from the war. It was decided to hold a competition, advertised worldwide, for a design to fit the specifications drawn up by the committee.

Several overseas entries were received, and after due consideration the committee decided that the entry of an expatriate New Zealander, Arthur Robb was the best. He was duly awarded first prize.

Bob Stewart had entered a design for a yacht measuring 11.6 m overall, 8.2 m on the waterline, 2.6 m in beam, 1.7 m in draught, with a displacement of 6.1 tonnes. She had a working sail area of 55 sq m — she was Bermudian sloop-rigged, but she had a genoa of 27 sq m and a spinnaker as extras. Construction details called for kauri planking on the three-skin diagonal principle, with teak trim and sitka spruce spars, and three tonnes of lead on the keel. The profile showed well proportioned lines, with a graceful sheer and a long coach house (dubbed "dog house" by local yachtsmen) over the companion way steps.

The Bob Stewart entry gained second place, and two other local designers — Bill Couldrey and Jack Brooke — were highly commended. Not undaunted by being only runner-up, Bob Stewart commissioned Colin Wild to build his entry. The yacht was named *Helen*.

Helen proved an immediate success, and was the first of the squadron K-class, being given sail number K.1. Other yachts built to the K-class specifications followed. Bill Couldrey designed and built the *Thelma* and *Jenanne*, and Colin Wild designed and built the *Kitenui* and *Dolita* (since renamed *Robin*). The class continued to expand through the 1950s: Bob Stewart designed the *Penelope* and *Katrina*, and McGruer of Scotland designed the *Anthea II* — the last yacht built by Collings and Bell at St. Mary's Bay before their yard was demolished in 1958 to make way for the Auckland Harbour Bridge motorway.

Jack Brooke altered the Arch Logan-designed, Couldrey-built *Waiomo*, launched in 1938, to meet the class specifications. With this experience Brooke then designed for himself the well-performed *Kiariki*. The last K-class vessel

built was designed by the renowned American designer Olin Stephens for Russ Hooper; she was christened *Sapphire*.

It is interesting to note that the prize-winning design by Arthur Robb was never built.

It is very doubtful that any more K-class yachts will be built, because their general design has today been superseded by the beamy, light, fibreglass-constructed, ocean racing type of yacht. A great pity, because the K-class fleet sailing together was a most attractive sight.

The K-class also gained a "snobby" reputation; no less than four yachts of this class have flown the commodore's pennant of the yacht squadron since the late 1950s. They have been *Anthea II* from 1957 to 1959 for Mr J. S. Ellis, *Katrina* from 1959 to 1961 for Mr J. F. Faire, *Waiomo* from 1961 to 1963 for Mr G. D. Speight and *Kiariki* from 1969 to 1971 for Mr Jack Brooke.

Other designers were active in the immediate post-war period, and notable among them was Eric Cox of Christchurch. Mr Cox was English-born, a draughtsman by profession, and his designs showed the meticulous work of such a professional. His designs were popular in southern waters, naturally enough, but even in Auckland, where few South Island designers have achieved prominence, there were some well-known and well-performed Cox designs built. Two of these were launched in 1948, both being built by Lidgard Brothers. One was *Teal*, 12.2 m overall, and the other was the fin keeler *Snow Goose*, 8.5 m overall (but later extended to 9.7 m).

Perhaps the largest Cox design built was the ketch *Red Feather*, a double ender which measured 15.2 m overall, 12.2 m on the waterline and 3.2 m in beam. She was built for a Canterbury yachtsman; cruising off the Canterbury coast some years ago she had the misfortune to have the skipper fall overboard and drown, leaving an inexperienced crew to sail her back to Lyttelton. Other Cox-designed yachts were the *Takohe*, a 12.2 m yawl, and *Wayleggo*, a 12.2 cutter. Together with *Red Feather*, these yachts took part in the 1966 Auckland to Suva yacht race and performed very well. This classic blue-water event was marred that year by the loss of the *Tatariki* and the withdrawal of several other yachts, such as *Fandango*, which were damaged in the cyclone which hit the racing fleet off North Cape (see chapter 13).

Until the 1950s, yacht design had been rea-

The K-class *Sapphire* makes a pretty picture as she slogs up the Waitemata in a fresh southerly.

Right: A fine example of a Hauraki Gulf cruiser. The Eric Cox-designed *Snow Goose* beats into a northerly in the Rangitoto Channel in 1956. She was later lengthened by nearly 2 m.

sonably stable. Relatively narrow beam and deep draught yachts of kauri construction predominated and it was found that they best countered the short, steep seas found on the New Zealand coast. This design trend had also been affected by the English, who experienced similar conditions around their coastlines. However the middle 1950s were to see enormous changes in yacht design and construction; this revolution will be discussed in the next chapter.

The third division keeler *Mercury* is a fine example of modern developments in the cruiser-racing yacht. This type of yacht combines both competitive racing and cruising comfort.

The modern way to handle boats. A new keeler being launched at Birkenhead ramp on Auckland harbour.

12.

The yachting revolution

IT IS DIFFICULT to state exactly why the whole direction of New Zealand yachting changed around the middle 1950s. It cannot be traced to one single factor. The causes lie in a whole combination of factors ranging from changing social habits to more mundane technical things like the development of reliable waterproof glues.

One certainty, however, was the interest and participation of women in a sport which up to that time had been solely, with one or two minor exceptions, a male preserve.

Yachting in New Zealand had always from the very first been the sport of the wealthy or at least the moderately wealthy; the crews were from the "better" families. Very few of the professional crewmen common in England took part in New Zealand yachting; the crews were drawn from fellow club members or their sons — enthusiasts who may not have had the money or inclination to own a yacht, but did have the interest. Young men usually joined the crew of a large keeler as soon as they left school. They served an "apprenticeship" as galley boys and bottle openers, graduating to sheet hands in the cockpit and then, if judged good enough, to the holy of holies — the fore-deck.

This transition would take five or six seasons, during which time the budding yachtsman learnt his craft thoroughly, and (just as importantly) developed a pride in the yacht he was privileged to sail on. It must also be remembered that this crew activity was a 12-month operation. Sailing took place from October (traditionally the launching date for each season was Labour Weekend) to April, while repairs and maintenance for the new season were carried out through the winter. Women and other sport took second place to the yacht.

Many old crewmen sailed on the one yacht through their entire crewing careers. When the owner decided to sell and either buy a larger yacht or else have a new one built, the whole crew went with him. Loyalty to the "skipper" and the yacht was total, a most marked contrast to the crew scene today.

This tradition still lingers. One crewman on the mighty *Ranger* has sailed on her since her launching 40 years ago. But as every year passes this old custom becomes more rare, and it is not hard to envisage a time when no more of these old-time crewmen are left.

The growing interest of women in yachting had one major result — yachts became more easy to live in. Women demanded, and got, more space, more light and more conveniences. The pre-war yachts were dark narrow tunnels below, particularly the flush-deck keelers built by the Logans — they were great for deck work, but uncomfortable to live in. Privacy was nonexistent, as were toilet facilities. The rigs were large and without modern aids such as winches; being difficult and heavy to handle they demanded large, fit and young male crews. The only time women went yachting was on what was quaintly called "cake days" — a gentle Sunday sail to Waiheke, when the women sat where they were told and did little but beautify the scene.

World War II finished all this. Women worked in jobs undreamed of to that time. They drove trucks or operated lathes, because of the manpower shortage, and when peace was restored they were not prepared to return to their servile roles. The returning serviceman also broke down traditional yachting customs. They wanted their own boat. Crewing wasn't enough. However money was still a problem, and the young ex-soldier had to get his priorities right. First he had to adapt to a peacetime job, then build his house — and then his boat.

Coinciding with this trend was the introduction of marine-grade plywood utilising glues developed for the building of wartime aircraft. Now it was possible to afford a yacht built in the backyard or under the house. But these new

94

materials required new designers, men capable of combining the products of a new technological age with the new conveniences which the wives of the budding builders demanded.

Seeing this trend, a young Wellington man studying architecture (but more interested in yachting) moved to Auckland in 1954; in a most humble way he set up business in a shed behind a service station in Devonport as a yacht designer and builder. This man was John Spencer, and his revolutionary ideas did more to change yacht design (not only in New Zealand but throughout the world) than any other designer in the 1950s and 60s. Even today in the late 1970s his influence is still felt in yacht design and construction.

John Spencer was quick to realise that flat sheets of plywood would not bend as readily and effectively as steamed planks or the skins of 6.3 or 12.7 mm timber which make up the diagonal-planked yachts. Sheets of plywood would not accept a compound curve; in reality they were best suited to a box with square ends — but such a shape will not sail successfully. With his architect training and draughtsman's skill with lines, Spencer pondered long on this problem. He decided he could overcome this reluctance of sheets of plywood to adapt to the fine entry and flowing flat runs aft necessary for a fast sailing boat. Above all he wanted to design pretty boats, combining all the features the typical yachtsman and his wife demanded. In addition they had to be easy to build; the yachtsman and his lady wanted to be able to build them at home, with a minimum of skill, tools and money.

Spencer realised that these radical ideas needed to be proved, and in 1954 he drew up the lines of a 3.6 m, two person yacht; it had a beam of 2.9 m and a working sail area of 9.3 sq m in a mainsail and jib. A spinnaker would be set when reaching or running. Spencer knew that the old traditional designs of New Zealand small-class yachts were too slow, too heavy and too expensive to build. He knew that the new generation wanted a light, cheap yacht which readily planed and was exciting to sail with the for'ard hand swinging from the trapeze.

He named the first boat from this design *Cherub*, building her in his shed behind the Devonport service station. He also broke with tradition and did not request a class symbol of an alphabetical letter. He merely put a heart on the sail — perhaps a symbol of his love affair with his new creation.

What the class was designed for. A Rothmans father and son class yacht reaching comfortably with a father and son aboard.

Traditional yachtsmen looked at the new boat with dismay. "It will not suit New Zealand conditions," they said. But how wrong they were. The *Cherub* sailed beyond even Spencer's expectations. Very soon the plans were in demand from all over New Zealand, and John Spencer was becoming quickly recognised as the first of a new generation of designers.

In the two decades since the first *Cherub* was sailed off the Devonport beach, nearly 2000 of these yachts have been built, 90 percent of them by amateurs. The design was also readily accepted by foreign yachtsmen, and today it can be regarded as New Zealand's major contribution to international yachting. Cherubs are built and sailed in Britain, Australia, America, Hong Kong and even Poland and Rhodesia.

The immediate success of the Cherub class spurred John Spencer to design other small-class yachts. The 3.2 m Flying Ant class was designed as a two-boy or father and son boat. It was designed as a trainer, and has a mainsail and jib totalling 6.3 sq m plus a spinnaker. This was followed by the Junior Cherub, which had a Cherub hull with a lower aspect ratio rig of the same sail area, which makes it easier and safer for the young yachtsman. The next design from Spencer was the 4.2 m Javelin — which is really a bigger and faster Cherub, having a 50 percent greater sail area. As we saw in an earlier chapter, the Javelin proved the ideal replacement for the outmoded T Y and X-class yachts. In fact the coveted Sanders Cup, formally competed for by the X-class, is now the national Javelin trophy.

All John Spencer designs incorporated lightness combined with strength, utilising plywood and modern glues. He realised that weight takes power to move: reduce the weight and more power is available. In sailing terms this means reduced sail areas, which means reduced costs without sacrificing speed — a desirable feature for yachtsmen on a limited budget.

Yachtsmen now began to ask whether this theory, now proven in small-boat design, would work in keelers. Spencer would not be hurried,

and gave considerable thought to such a design. The result basically exploited the lessons learnt with the Cherub. Lightness associated with strength was again the key, and the first keeler design was hard chined with a fine entrance and the good run characteristic of all Spencer yachts. These lines ensured maximum speed reaching or running, with a deep plate keel providing good stability for windward work. The first Spencer keelers included such well-known boats as *Scimitar*, *Sirocco* and the *Saracen*. The last-named was built for a newcomer to yachting, Auckland industrialist Tom Clark — who had previously been better known as a racing car driver. Tom Clark learnt his keeler sailing in *Saracen*, and achieved considerable success with her in both harbour and passage races. But like her sister ships, *Saracen* was only 10.6 m overall, and Tom Clark wanted to get into first division racing. So he approached John Spencer to design and build for him a yacht "capable of beating *Ranger*".

The result was the magnificent *Infidel*, certainly the fastest yacht designed by Spencer. In fact at the time of her launching in 1965 she was the largest hard chine plywood keeler in the world. John Spencer had earlier stated that the *Saracen* was but the prototype for a much larger boat, and *Infidel* was that boat.

Tom Clark's specifications to John Spencer were for a big, fast yacht with comfortable accommodation for eight, but ample room on

Infidel — the "black box" — without doubt John Spencer's greatest design, here weaving her way through a mixed fleet. Astern are Flying Dutchmen, while ahead are *Nomad* (A.47) and *St. George* (C.7).

deck for a large number of guests for day sailing, and a simple, efficient rig. The length was determined by the overall length of Spencer's workshop. The result was a yacht which measured 18.8 m overall, 15.4 m on the waterline, 3.5 m in beam, with a draft of 2.7 m and a displacement of 10 tonnes. The sail area was moderate for a yacht of this size, the mainsail being of 66.8 sq m, the genoa 74 sq m, and No.1 jib 56.6 sq m, the No.2 jib 37 sq m and the spinnaker 232 sq m.

With the exception of the fittings and some finishing John Spencer built her single-handed. The hull was constructed from sheet plywood using two skins, each of 9.52 mm thickness, over stringers laminated on the bottom, spanning a system of bulkheads and laminated intermediate floors through the main part of the boat, with conventional frames in the ends, thus providing immense strength compared with conventional methods of construction.

The deck beams were incorporated into the frames and bulkheads, with fore and aft stringers over these in the ends. The deck was 15.9 mm thick, consisting of one skin of 9.52 mm and one skin of 6.35 mm plywood. The coamings were 22.20 mm thick, being cut back to provide rebates for the perspex windows, which were held in by stainless steel rims. The cabin top was laminated to shape over temporary formers from one lamination of 9.52 mm and two of 4.76 mm plywood. She was thus free of beams inside. The hatch runners for the large aluminium alloy hatches acted as fore and aft girders, all the hatches being sliding.

Another innovation Spencer adopted was the large for'ard cockpit, which allowed more efficient headsail changing and general foredeck work. Both this for'ard cockpit and the main cockpit were self-draining. The main cockpit, which was 3.6 m long, was divided into two by a central bridge which carried the mainsheet track and winch and also housed the speedometer, windspeed and direction indicator and depth sounder. Immediately aft of this was the instrument panel for the auxiliary motor, which is a Universal Atomic Four motor with an Aqua-Pak drive, with a two:one reduction driving a 15 x 12 folding propeller.

In a yacht so trend-setting it was surprising that John Spencer fitted a tiller, instead of the usual alloy destroyer-type steering wheel so favoured by other designers. Aft of the main cockpit was the after hatch which opened to a further cockpit from which the spinnaker after guy and sheet were handled. Below decks *Infidel* was designed to be comfortable as well as efficient. The hull was floored from end to end almost full width between the chines, which in the stern section therefore gave an ideal area for stowage and also additional sleeping space if required. Ports in the cockpit sides gave ample light and ventilation. There were eight bunks and normal galley facilities, including a refrigerator (an essential commodity with a big crew).

Infidel was launched painted black with a broad white boot-topping, a colour scheme Tom Clark has used for all his yachts. In fact because of this colour *Infidel* came to be known affectionately amongst yachtsmen as the "black box". In her first season, 1965-66, she proved her paper potential. A notable success was at the 1966 Auckland Anniversary Regatta, when she was first home in an A-class fleet which included *Ranger* and *Fidelis*, by over nine minutes. In the Auckland to Russell Christmas cruising race, which ended in gale conditions, she completed the 193 km course in under 14 hours, one and a half hours ahead of the next boat. In the Kawau Island weekend conducted by the Royal New Zealand Yacht Squadron in February 1966 she won three times in three races, including the night race to Kawau, (which she sailed in two hours 20 minutes, at that time a record performance).

Infidel proved John Spencer's theories and established him as an international designer. She was the first yacht to challenge *Ranger* — over the five seasons from 1965 to 1970 neither yacht ever quite established supremacy over the other. It is of interest to record here the vital statistics and the time correction factors based on the performance of each yacht in the races conducted by the Royal New Zealand Yacht Squadron over the four seasons from 1966 to 1969.

	Length Overall (metres)	Length Waterline	Beam	Draft	Working Sail Area (square metres)	Displacement (tonnes)
Ranger	18.3	14	3.5	2.8	92.9	12.2
Infidel	18.8	15.4	3.5	2.7	123.5	10.1

TIME CORRECTION FACTORS:

	1966	1967	1968	1969
Ranger	.973	.988	.971	.980
Infidel	1.000	1.000	1.000	1.000

The cockpit of a champion. *Infidel*, with owner Tom Clark at the tiller, at the finish of yet another race. Six rolls in the mainsail indicate that conditions have been tough.

In 1970 Tom Clark decided to sell *Infidel* and to commission John Spencer to design a true ocean racer incorporating all the design and construction lessons learned from *Saracen* and *Infidel*. In spite of her record there was little local interest in *Infidel*, and she was purchased by a syndicate of American west coast yachtsmen for a reputed gift price of $30,000. She was renamed *Ragtime* and shipped to California, where she has since been resold several times, the last time for $U.S.120,000. Inflation is not the only factor responsible for this huge price increase. Although originally designed for Auckland harbour conditions, *Ragtime* has won two trans-Pacific races from Los Angeles to Honolulu (one in record time) beating on elapsed times such yachts as *Windward Passage* and *Kialoa*. Although he has not said it in public, Tom Clark admits that selling the "black box" — *Infidel* — was a great mistake.

John Spencer designed and built the schooner *New World* for American shipping magnate George Kissadon in 1969, and continued to build yachts for local yachtsmen.

His next big commission was the designing of *Infidel's* successor for Tom Clark. The instructions were simple — a bigger and better *Infidel*, which could sail the oceans of the world and would rate well under the new I.O.R. rules of measurement.

The only similarities between *Infidel* and the new vessel *Buccaneer* were their plywood construction and colour schemes. *Buccaneer* measured a massive 22.2 m overall, with a beam of 4.9 m and a draft of 3.2 m.

It is hard to assess *Buccaneer*. She was not designed as a harbour racer and indeed has been soundly beaten by smaller yachts such as *Ranger*, *Ta'aroa* and *Fidelis* (as well as having also beaten them on occasions). Yet her ocean racing performance has also not been great; she proved to be underpowered compared with American champions such as *Kialoa*, and *Windward Passage* — the same yachts *Infidel* has beaten in blue water races. Perhaps *Buccaneer's* greatest win was in the year she was launched, in the 1970 Sydney to Hobart race when she was actually still being tuned up during the race.

Infidel must remain John Spencer's greatest design, although in very recent years Wellington fliers such as *Whispers of Wellington* and *Aztec* have continued to prove the genius of this gifted New Zealand designer and builder.

Other designers have also come to the fore. Bob Stewart, whose early designs were discussed in the previous chapter, quickly realised the potential of light displacement moulded yachts, and in 1960 designed the 10.3 m *Patiki* for Mr Peter Colmore-Williams. Stewart readily admits the influence of mullet boats in his decision to

Buccaneer reaches up to the finish of the annual Auckland to Bay of Islands race. Tom Clark can be seen on the wheel concentrating on the set of the genoa.

replace the centreboard with a fin keel, and to place a spade-rudder as far aft as possible. Wetted surface was reduced to a minimum, and with big bilges, a flat run and lots of power, the design fairly screamed "speed". And so it proved. *Patiki* was built by John Lidgard and launched for the 1960-61 season. She proved an immediate success and was quickly followed by others of the same design. Today there are nearly 30 of these fine little keelers racing in the Stewart 34 class, as they are now called.

Bob Stewart went on to design bigger yachts such as *Northerner*, *Carmen* and *Myth of Arran* — all were variations on the *Patiki* theme and all were successful yachts. *Northerner* built by Max Carter for Boyd Hargraves, measured 15.2 m

overall; in her first two seasons she proved very fast, beating such yachts as *Ranger*, *Kahurangi* and *Fidelis*. However she hit Bollons Rock off Tiri Tiri Island during a Balokovic Cup race and sank. She was recovered and repaired, but never again proved the yacht she was in her first two seasons.

John Lidgard, well-known in Auckland yachting as a builder, has also achieved a great deal of success as a designer. His designs, drawn up especially for Hauraki Gulf conditions, have proved most successful. Yachts such as *Takiri* and her sister ships *Taonui*, which competed with success in several ocean races, and the one-tonner *Runaway* have established his name as a designer of fine seakindly yachts.

Jim Young is another builder-turned-designer who has also been regarded as an innovator. His first yacht was the very fine double-ender *Fiery Cross*, designed by the American Herreshoff, but with Young adaptations. This trend-setter had a swinging keel designed to swing to the windward side of the boat and so improve stability, but it was outlawed for racing and the idea was never really proven. Jim

Young's yachts are characterised by light displacement, low wetted surface, fin keel, light scantlings and big sail areas, requiring good crews to really get the best out of them.

His first venture into designing was the red-hulled *Tango* in 1956, which was followed by the *Shemara* for Bernie Schmidt. Both yachts proved very competitive, and *Shemara*, which is today in Wellington, has won many races. These were followed by Warwick Wrightson's 11 m

A mixed bag of Stewart 34s, first division keelers and smaller yachts lie becalmed while frustrated crews stand on their foredecks and try to decide from where the next puff is coming from.

Spencer's *Whispers of Wellington*, owned by Geoff Stagg of Wellington, hard on the wind and moving fast.

two-master *Secret II* another fast yacht.

However the next Young design was the one which really proved his designing skill. This was the 11.3 m *Namu*, owned and sailed so capably by "Flap" Martinengo. *Namu* has proved virtually unbeatable by yachts of her size, and proved the prototype of the New Zealand 37 class, many of which have been exported to the United States. Jim Young's venture into the one-ton cuppers was the radical *Checkmate*, a potentially very fast yacht which has been plagued by "teething problems". His latest creations are the Young 43s, a luxury 13 m design which is available in a variety of options depending on the owner's interests but is basically a fast motor-sailer.

A good example of a designer proving himself in small-class racers before moving into the keeler classes is Des Townsen. He first achieved success sailing the 2.1 m P-class, then graduated into the unrestricted Q-class (3.6 m), where many "way-out" design trends are experimented with. In 1954 Townsen designed the Q-class yacht *Nimble*, which in 1956 was adopted by the Tamaki Yacht Club as the one-design monotype Zephyr — of which over 300 have been built. This was followed in 1959 by the *Mistral*, a slightly longer two-man yacht carrying both a headsail and a spinnaker. In 1961 he designed the *Dart*, a 3.3 m square chine plywood two-boy yacht, which was sailed mainly by the Waiuku Sailing Club.

Like John Spencer, Des Townsen wanted to also design fast, light displacement keelers. His first effort, *Serene*, proved very successful and several yachts to this design were launched. Then followed *Pied Piper* and *Mercia*, both 6.7 m, and *Tamahere*, an enlarged *Serene*. He then moved into larger yachts, and the 9.5 m *Magic Flute* was launched. Like her predecessors she proved fast, but she lacked displacement — particularly in a hard bash to windward. Still learning, Townsen designed the heavier displacement, 9.7 m *Moonlight*, which sailed by the redoubtable Peter Mulgrew in the 1971 One Ton Cup trials proved a sensation. She very nearly sneaked into third place, which would have displaced *Young Nick*, the latest creation of the then doyens of One Ton Cup design, Sparkman and Stephens. Many more fast yachts will come from Des Townsen's drawing board.

Another prominent Auckland designer is Laurie Davidson, who first made his name in the centreboard classes, particularly the 5.5 m M-

class, and then moved onto quarter and half-tonners such as *Blitzkrieg* for Tony Bouzaid. Another is Alan Warwick, who sailed with Chris Bouzaid in the famous one-tonner *Rainbow II*, and then skippered *Young Nick* for Mr Lou Fisher in the 1971 series. Warwick has designed a most interesting 19.5 m yacht, which looks capable of challenging Auckland's first division racing fleet. Richard Hartley, who specialises in designing trailer-sailers for amateur builders, "Bo" Birdsall, who has designed mullet boats and very fast keelers such as *Rhubarb* and *Venus*, and Owen Woolley, whose 7.9 m Ravens are

The Bob Stewart designed Stewart 34 class, here lie becalmed, while their crews set spinnakers, in an effort to catch every puff of wind, during a R.N.Z.Y.S. race in 1972.

Innismara is one of the many fine yachts designed and built by amateur yachtsmen, in this case Bernie Schmidt. This fine stern shot shows the broad stern and narrow beam of this fast first division keeler.

The race is on. The Bob Stewart-designed *Northerner* in the foreground as Auckland keelers set spinnakers. The *Northerner's* crew are stowing the genoa.

very well-known, have all contributed to the development of New Zealand yachting — and will continue to do so.

There are also other designers who are coming to the fore but who in this age of specialisation tend to concentrate on one particular type of design. John Gladden and Allan Mummery have made a name for themselves in the design of fast, good looking bilge keelers, a design type particularly suited to tidal estuary conditions because of their shoal-draught. Phillip Atkinson, still in his twenties, has designed ultra-modern quarter-tonners such as the wedge-shaped multi-chined *Demon Tweaker*. Atkinson got his start in yacht designing by winning the Royal Akarana Yacht Club's design scholarship for the yacht design course at the Auckland

Technical Institute. He is another young designer who promises to have a marked effect on the future of New Zealand yachting.

Two southern designers have also attracted attention in recent years. One is Hal Wagstaff of Wellington, who in 1974 retired from his architecture practice to become a full-time yacht designer. Wagstaff is well-known for the design of stock hulls known as Harmonics — the Harmonic 24, a quarter-tonner, and the Harmonic 30, a half-tonner. He has also produced a stock trailer-sailer, the Mallard 22. The other southern designer is Trevor Adams of Christchurch, who after working as a warehouseman studied at the Auckland Technical Institute where he won the top design award for his year.

A Whangarei designer, Claude Smith, has also risen to prominence in recent years, with two designs which are now stock hulls, produced in fibreglass. The first of these is the 9.1 m *Eas-*

terly, which is a round bilge, moderate displacement fin keeler. With a beam of 3 m on a 7.3 m waterline, it gives ample room below for a crew of five. His other well-known design, the Pacific 38, has also been well received by local yachtsmen as a fast, comfortable cruiser.

Alan Wright is a local designer who has produced a range of designs from the 6.1 m Tasman trailer-sailer to a 20.1 m motor-sailer. He has catered to the stock boat market with craft such as the 6.8 m *Variant*, manufactured in fibreglass, and has also created plans for the amateur builder — such as the Wright 36, of which the twin-keel *Nerissa* is a fine example.

Other designers such as Graeme McCaw of Christchurch, Bruce Askew of Wellington, Don Brooke (son of Jack Brooke), John Woollacott (son of the late Bert Woollacott), Edward Ewbank, Brian Donovan, all of Auckland, and Erwin Haag of Whangarei, all offer custom design facilities to would-be yacht owners.

Perhaps the best known Auckland builders who are also yacht designers are the Salthouse brothers, who have their yard at the top end of the Waitemata Harbour at Greenhithe. The Salthouse brothers pioneered the stock yacht concept in New Zealand back in the middle

The Jim Young-designed *Secret II* competing in the ice-breaker race on a stormy Waitemata Harbour in October 1971.

1960s. Up to that time all keeler construction was of the "one off" technique, but it was becoming obvious that to keep the price of boats in the reach of all the overseas concept of "factory" production of a one-class yacht must be introduced. The introduction of fibreglass meant that many hulls could be taken from a master mould, allowing this stock boat one-class principle to become a practical possibility.

The first class developed in this way was the Cavalier 32, designed by Bob Salthouse, which was well accepted by New Zealand yachtsmen and proved very competitive in rating races, particularly when conditions were fresh. However the 9.76 m overall length was an awkward size in that it was too large for a half-ton rating and too small for the competitive one-ton fleet. The Cavalier 36, based on the *Ganbare* design of Doug Peterson, was then introduced, followed by the Cavalier 39, again designed by Bob Salthouse. At a later date the range was extended to include the Cavalier 26, a quarter-tonner, and the Cavalier 30, a half-tonner. These two yachts were again designed by Doug Peterson. The standard of finish of the Cavaliers has always been a hallmark; this is not surprising when it is considered that Bob Salthouse learnt his trade under the master craftsman Colin Wild, who was renowned for the finish of the yachts he constructed.

But there are three New Zealand yacht designers, all Aucklanders (one being an expatriate), who currently dominate not only the local design scene, but also the design of level rating classes throughout the world — particularly the quarter, half and one-ton categories. Now their influence is also being felt in the design of the two-ton category, the glamorous Admiral's Cup class.

These three designers are Ron Holland, who now lives and operates from Cork in Ireland, Bruce Farr and Paul Whiting. They are all under 30 years of age; each of these gifted young men is yet to reach the peak of his designing skill.

In terms of age Ron Holland is the senior, and provides the classic example of a practical yachtsman who turned designer and applied his practical skills to the drawing board. He is also a good example of the young New Zealander who gains a trade (Holland is a qualified boatbuilder) or profession and then leaves to obtain overseas experience in his chosen field. Ron Holland left New Zealand in 1970 for the United States, where he worked for prominent yacht designers and at the same time did a lot of sailing. He first came to international prominence when he sailed the New Zealand-built, but American Gary Mull-designed *Improbable*, in the Admiral's Cup races off Cowes in 1973.

Holland's first really big international success came in 1974, when *Eygthene* a quarter-tonner of his design won the World Quarter Ton Championship, held that year in England. At this time Holland, who married an American girl, was living in the United States, but he was commissioned by an Irish yachtsman, Hugh Coveney, to design a one-tonner for him. He flew to Ireland to see the prospective owner, and was so impressed with the south of Ireland (which is also geographically central to the yachting centres of the Northern Hemisphere) that he decided to set up his design office in the city of Cork. The one-tonner turned out to be *Golden Apple*, and after the success of this yacht the distinctive *Golden* prefix for the names of Holland-designed yachts has become a trademark. Examples are *Golden Shamrock* and *Golden Dazy* and in New Zealand the fast quarter-tonner *Golden Kiwi*, owned by Gil Hedges, who previously owned *Escapade*.

Surprisingly, Holland's designs have not proved particularly popular with New Zealand yachtsmen. This is due perhaps to the lack of success he has achieved in the One Ton Cup class. Chris Bouzaid's successes in 1969 and 1972, have made this the "hot" rating, and designer's skills are now measured by their performance in this level rating class. However the Holland-designed *Measure for Measure* won the 1975 New Zealand Half-Ton Championship, beating a host of international and local designs.

Ron Holland's designs are regarded as light displacement. The majority are being built in aluminium, which gives the best rigidity for weight. However he is also investigating the utilisation of carbon fibre with wood laminates, which offers the possibility of further reducing weight in hull construction without sacrificing strength. Carbon fibre is also being used in the building of masts, where the same advantages exist. There is also the possibility of getting mast bend exactly where it is wanted, using hydraulics on all the rigging, not only on the forestay and backstay as currently used.

Ron Holland has certainly placed New Zealand well on the world map as a force in design development, and it is hoped that one day he will return to the land of his birth to

Perhaps one of the busiest yards in New Zealand. Salthouse Brothers yard on the upper reaches of the Waitemata Harbour.

encourage and educate young local designers and builders in the demanding field of international yacht design and construction.

The next senior designer of international repute, in terms of age, is Bruce Farr. Although his career has been similar to Holland's in terms of practical application, it has differed in that he has not ventured overseas to learn further skills and attract international clients. If anything, the clients have come to him.

Bruce Farr came into yacht-designing in a fashion similar to that pioneered by John Spencer some years before. He is a mathematical draughtsman who applied his advanced theories to small-yacht design, where they were proven, before venturing into the more demanding area of keelboat design. Farr first came to local and national attention when he designed the 3.7 m-class yacht, a demanding, exciting, one-man-on-trapeze craft which proved very popular with the more agile, fitter yachtsman. Nearly 200 have been built, primarily by amateurs.

The unrestricted racing 18-footers (5.5 m) next attracted Farr's attention. At one stage practically the whole Australasian fleet of "eighteens" were Farr-designed boats, so superior were they to other designs. This Farr domination reached a peak at the 1974 World 18-footer Championships held at Auckland, when the *Travelodge New Zealand*, designed by Farr and sailed brilliantly by Terry McDell, Peter Brook and Kim McDell, not only won the invitation race but went on to win four straight victories, the first win by New Zealanders in New Zealand waters since 1960. This clear-cut victory was achieved in the face of hot Australian competition from the experienced Sydney skipper Dave Porter and his boat *K.B.*. Third in the series was *Captain Morgan*, a John Chappel design skippered by Wayne Innes of New Zealand.

Bruce Farr had served his apprenticeship in yacht design in these classes and was now ready to challenge the world's best in the level rating classes. Following his policy of working up to

Prospect of Ponsonby jockeying for position at the start of the final race of the 1975 Southern Cross Cup trials.

The Bruce Farr-designed 18-footer *Miss UEB* chases *Crown Lynn* during a race on Auckland harbour in 1975.

the big classes, the half-ton (9.1 m overall) yachts first attracted his attention. His first design for this class was the phenomenal *Titus Canby*, which attracted the attention of not only the yachting public but all the public of New Zealand with her great win on the inaugural South Pacific Half-Ton Trophy in 1972. This little boat, only 8.11 m overall, was renamed *Tohe Candu* when she was purchased by Ponsonby Cruising Club member Ian Gibbs. She again won the Schweppes New Zealand and South Pacific Half-Ton Trophy from a 33-boat fleet, including three Australian crews. After this win Gibbs took *Tohe Candu* to the World Half-Ton Championship in France, but did not achieve the success expected.

However Bruce Farr produced a design for the quarter-ton rating class (7.3 m overall) which was to really bring him into the very top flight of international designers. This design became known as the Farr 727. Two yachts of this design, the *727*, skippered by Farr himself, and the *Genie*, skippered by former *Pathfinder* and *Inca* skipper Roy Dickson, fought out the 1975 Pacific Quarter-Ton contest. A fleet of 31 boats entered the four races (including a 322 km offshore event) but the two Farr sister ships proved unbeatable with the *727* winning with a second-first-first-fourth tally. However controversy clouded the result when *Genie* was disqualified in the intermediate (96 km) ocean race "for the incorrect placing of an anchor". But for this disqualification *Genie* would have won this hotly contested series.

108

The revolutionary *Prospect of Ponsonby*, designed by Bruce Farr and owned by Noel Angus — here at the helm. This was her first race, which she won easily and thus established Farr as a hot keel-boat designer as well as a centreboard wizard.

Undaunted, Roy Dickson took the *Genie* to La Rochelle in France, where after a brilliant display of eased sheet sailing in the English Channel, she won for New Zealand the World Quarter-Ton Trophy. Bruce Farr had proved his designing skill in international competition.

The question was now whether Farr would prove just as good in the more challenging one-ton class. The answer was soon forthcoming. On paper the design looked fast, with all the Farr trademarks — the distinctive knuckle bow, the rather slab-sided freeboard in the for'ard section, the three-quarter rig and the very light displacement. Overall she measured 11 m on the waterline, 3.6 m in beam, 1.7 m in draft. The displacement was 4080 kg and the ballast weighed 1547 kg.

The first yacht launched was the exuberantly named *Prospect of Ponsonby*. Her owner and

skipper, Noel Angus, was an experienced yachtsman in both round-the-buoy and offshore racing, having crewed in many of Auckland's top keelers. He had recently owned the Canadian-designed *Mustang*, which had been built to contest the 1971 One Ton Cup trials. *Mustang* was not tuned for the trials because of a lack of time from launching to the trial series, and did not perform to her full potential. But she was finally chartered by a Canadian crew, and skippered by John Beatson she finished a creditable 11th overall in an extremely competitive fleet of 17 boats.

Prospect of Ponsonby was launched in September 1975 and immediately commenced tuning up for her first big challenge, the 1975 Southern Cross trials, in an effort to make the New Zealand team to contest the 1975 Southern Cross Cup, to be held in Sydney. The world's yachtsmen waited to see how the latest Farr creation would perform against top designs from such esteemed designers as Gary Mull, Sparkman and Stephens, and Ron Holland.

They were not disappointed. Capably skippered and crewed, *Prospect of Ponsonby* made a clean sweep of the trials, gaining five firsts from five races. It appeared that Bruce Farr had again designed a champion, but this trial form needed to be proved in international competition. This came when she sailed across the Tasman to Sydney, together with two other New Zealand representatives, to contest the coveted Southern Cross Cup.

It is history now that the *Prospect of Ponsonby* did indeed prove the Farr design against the world's best. She was top boat of the series, gaining two firsts, one second and one third, in the process beating the then current world One Ton Cup-holder *Pied Piper*, designed by Doug Peterson from the United States. *Prospect of Ponsonby* did not return to New Zealand, being sold to an Australian yachtsman.

Back in New Zealand, the Bruce Farr one-ton designs had become the hottest property around. With the Dunhill Classic series and the One Ton Cup championship to be held in Marseilles in France in 1976, top skippers clamoured for the champion Farr-designed boats. Two of these yachts attracted the greatest attention. They were *Jiminy Cricket*, owned and sailed by Stuart Brentnall (who had previously owned and raced a Stewart 34), and *The Number*, skippered by Graeme Woodroffe (who was a very well-known and experienced centreboard yachtsman — his crew were likewise all small-boat men). *The Number* was not launched in time for the Dunhill Classic series, but *Jiminy Cricket* took part, and convincingly won the $2000 prize for the overall winner, having two firsts, one second and a third from four races.

As we shall see in chapter 14, *The Number* narrowly beat *Jiminy Cricket* in an exciting One Ton Cup trial series, and an appeal for public funds resulted in both yachts being sent to Marseilles. In chapter 14 we examine how the two New Zealand yachts performed superbly but finally failed to recapture the cup last won by Chris Bouzaid in 1972.

Bruce Farr's reputation was not damaged by the result of the 1976 one-ton series. His designs finished second and third, and he picked up one lesson learnt by all designers — that each series location requires a "horses for courses" approach. Already Farr has modified his one-ton design, and the first of the second generation designs, *Country Boy*, has been launched. In April 1977 *Country Boy*, sailed by Clyde Colson, became the top New Zealand one-tonner by winning all four races in the national One-Ton Championships, sailed off Auckland.

Bruce Farr has also turned his attention to the Admiral's Cup-type yachts, the so-called two-tonners of 12.80 m overall. His first design was the very well performed *Gerontius*, owned and sailed by Grahame Eder, which very surprisingly beat the Sparkman and Stephens-designed *Corinthian* (built without regard for cost by Auckland industrialist Russ Hooper) for third place in the three-yacht New Zealand team which took part in the Admiral's Cup competition held on the Solent in England in August 1975. The other team members were *Inca*, owned and skippered by Evan Julian, and *Barnacle Bill*, owned by Ron Jarden and sailed by Ray Haslar. Both yachts were designed by Sparkman and Stephens. A report on the Admiral's Cup races is contained in chapter 15.

New Zealand's first entry into the really big league of international yachting was not successful but Bruce Farr learnt a lot from the challenge, and is currently designing two-tonners for Paul Smith, an Adelaide yachtsman, and for a Hong Kong yachtsman. Both are intended to race in the 1978 Admiral's Cup contest. Both these yachts are being built to the latest technical specifications, utilising high strength glass laminates with carbon fibres to give the maximum stiffness with minimum weight. Stability has been sacrificed for more sail area, and both the freeboard and beam have been reduced compared with earlier designs. The performance of these yachts will be watched with great interest.

Bruce Farr has in a short time established

Another Bruce Farr design — the *Kailua*, owned by John Senior, here reaching down Whangarei Harbour. The sheer power of the Farr boats is evident in this photograph.

The power of the Bruce Farr-designed *Gerontius*, here sailing the waters of the Solent in England during the second inshore race for the Admiral's Cup in 1975, is very apparent in this photograph.

Darcy Whiting's *Tequila*, designed by his son Paul, "on the hard" at Westhaven. She shows the modern trend in yacht design — a fin keel, independent spade rudder, flat midsection and long run aft.

himself as a yacht designer equal to if not better than any in the world. It would appear that to maintain this reputation he will be forced to move overseas to be closer to the major yachting centres, a move which Ron Holland has found to be so advantageous. When and if this happens, New Zealand will lose an extremely gifted yacht designer.

The junior member (in terms of age) of this talented trio is Paul Whiting, a member of a well-known Auckland yachting family. His father, Darcy Whiting, has sailed and raced the Hauraki Gulf and offshore waters for many years, first in his well known yacht *Coruba*, then more recently in *Tequila*. His sister, Penny Whiting, has taken part in several classic offshore races and has taught many New Zealanders to sail in the sailing school she operates from her John Spencer-designed keeler *Avian* on the Waitemata Harbour.

Paul Whiting has sailed all his life, and like

111

both Holland and Farr has applied practical considerations to his yacht designs. As a young child he sailed with his father, and at 16 years of age designed the 11.6 m *Coruba*, which he and his father built at the back of their house. *Coruba* proved a husky offshore racer, taking part with some success in several blue water races. In 1973 *Coruba* was sold, and the young Whiting designed a 13.7 m cutter, again for his father, which was called *Tequila*. This yacht also proved successful in offshore racing, and in 1975 Darcy Whiting and his wife sailed on an extensive cruise throughout the Pacific and further afield.

Whiting really made his name when at the age of 18 he designed the 7.6 m *Reactor*. The prototype proved so successful that it was decided to produce a stock hull in fibreglass, and Whiting Yachts Ltd. was established. Today over 60 Reactors are afloat, and they are still being built. This success spurred the development of a larger keeler, and so the Reactor 45 was designed. It had an overall length of 13.5 m, measured 11.4 m on the waterline and 3.9 m in beam, with a draught of 2.4 m. The design is basically a

modified *Tequila*, but deeper in the bow sections and narrower in the stern (which means a considerably better rating). The hull is constructed from solid hand-laid fibreglass over close glass stringers, and is built in excess of the latest Lloyds specifications for fibreglass boats. The Reactor 45 is the largest yacht to be built to these specifications in New Zealand, and is one of the biggest stock boats available in the country.

But like Holland and Farr, Whiting's interest and talent for designing fast yachts was drawn to the rating classes and to the chance to match his skill in international series against the world's best designers.

Like Farr, Paul Whiting first designed a yacht to compete in the quarter-ton rating class. This yacht was the radical *Magic Bus*, which featured innovations in rig and deck layout. The rig was a three-quarter set-up, with a soft Baverstock mast, which bent with mainsheet tension, not backstay load. This meant that the full mainsail and No.1 genoa could be carried in wind gusts of up to 25 knots (when other yachts would be struggling or reefed down).

After a series of trial races in the Hauraki Gulf

Coruba, an early Paul Whiting design, reaches down Whangarei Harbour en route to Noumea in 1971.

A New Zealand world champion. Paul Whiting's great quarter-tonner *Magic Bus*.

in early 1976 *Magic Bus*, sailed extremely well by Murray Ross, a 26-year-old Auckland sailmaker, beat all the local quarter-tonners (including the latest Farr creation *Pinto*) to earn the right to represent New Zealand in the 1976 World Quarter-Ton Championship held at Corpus Christi, Texas. New Zealand was of course the defending champion, having won the title in 1975 in France with the Bruce Farr-designed *45 South*. (This yacht did not return to New Zealand; she was sold to an English yachtsman, who from 37 starts gained 27 firsts in the 1976 English summer.)

New Zealand had a big reputation to live up to, and the Whiting-designed *Magic Bus* did not disappoint. All the top designers were represented, with the main competition expected to come from a Ron Holland design called *Business Machine*, which represented America.

In light-wind conditions with a lumpy sea *Magic Bus* won the series again for New Zealand with a first-first-second-eighteenth-second tally from five starts. *Business Machine* had a tally of third-seventh-seventh-second-third to finish in second place. With every world designer represented, New Zealand designers thus took first and second place. The Laurie Davidson-designed *Fun*, a private entry sailed by Davidson, finished in fifth place with a second-sixth-tenth-twenty-first-fourth tally.

Paul Whiting had proved his talents in world class competition. Now his attentions will no doubt be drawn to the one-ton and two-ton classes.

With Ron Holland and Bruce Farr, Paul Whiting has established New Zealand as perhaps the world's top yacht-designing country. The greatest pity of this development is that there is not the money in this country to provide the new, radical extremely expensive materials such as carbon fibre, which these modern designers must use to remain competitive. It would appear that Farr and Whiting could well be forced to live in the Northern Hemisphere — like their counterpart Ron Holland — so that their very obvious potential can be realised to the absolute maximum.

New Zealand can justifiably be proud of these three young men who have proved their designing skills against the very best yacht-designers in the world. Ron Holland in particular has been internationally recognised by the request from the former British Prime Minister Edward Heath to design for him *Morning Cloud V*. She will be constructed from aluminium, measuring 13.4 m overall with a 3.9 m beam.

History has a habit of repeating itself. A century ago Robert Logan and Charles Bailey were designing fast yachts for English, South African and Australian owners. Today Ron Holland, Bruce Farr and Paul Whiting are doing the same.

13.

New Zealand yachting disasters

NEW ZEALAND is geographically unique, extending in a north-south direction for over 1600 km yet at its widest part stretching only 193 km from coast to coast. It is perhaps the most isolated country in the world, being 1900 km from its nearest neighbours, Australia to the west and Fiji to the north. Eastwards, the nearest land mass is the western shore of the South American continent, 9600 km distant, while to the south lie the grim icelands of Antarctica. The South Island lies across the westerly winds of the "roaring forties", while the North Island is lashed by sub-tropical cyclones at certain times of the year. Experienced yachtsmen and professional seamen have often stated that the seas around the New Zealand coast are among the worst in the world, and should be treated with great respect. So it is little wonder that since the development of yachting there have been several tragedies involving the loss of life off the New Zealand coast. .

The most perplexing and serious losses involving yachts have been in the Cook Strait region, that area of raging storms and huge breaking seas which develop so quickly, so often without warning. Three yachts, well-crewed by experienced seamen, have been lost in this area in the past 40 years, each loss capturing the attention of the New Zealand public. The first of these losses was the 7.9 m yawl *Windward*, in January 1931; the other two occurred during the tragic Wellington to Lyttelton yacht race in January 1951, when the yachts *Argo* and *Husky* were lost virtually without trace.

The inexplicable loss of the *Windward* remains one of New Zealand's great mysteries, both on sea and land. *Windward* was built in Wellington in 1911 by her first owner, Mr Ralph Millman. She measured 8 m overall, 2.6 m in the beam and 1.7 m in draught. She displaced six tonnes, having two tonnes of lead ballast on her keel. *Windward* was typical of the solid yachts designed and built for Cook Strait conditions,

having double-skinned kauri planking, copper fastened, with a keel hewn out of a massive piece of heart kauri. During the 20 years of her life *Windward* had proved a fast, seaworthy yacht, winning many trophies in races run by the Royal Port Nicholson Yacht Club and crossing Cook Strait to the Marlborough Sounds cruising grounds nearly every season.

At 8 a.m. on 25 December 1930 the *Windward* cleared the Wellington boat harbour on a cruise to the Chatham Islands and return. Her crew consisted of J. P. Rollings, skipper, C. A. Steele, A. H. Irwin and D. A. Graham. They were all students at Victoria University and experienced yachtsmen. The skipper was a graduate in mathematics and an expert navigator, while Graham was a lieutenant in the Royal Naval Volunteer Reserve and a qualified navigator.

Windward had been well prepared for the 640 km ocean passage, having new standing rigging, running gear and storm sails. In addition she carried a new sea anchor, two oil bags and a drum of oil, and was fully equipped with a good compass, complete set of charts, sextant, chronometer, tested barometer, patent log and a radio receiver with a direction-finder in place of the local speaker. She was sufficiently fitted out to make a world voyage and was provisioned with 181 litres of water, medical necessities and ample food supplies.

On the outward passage *Windward* covered the 640 km in seven days, arriving at Waitangi in the Chathams on New Years Day 1931. During this passage she was hove-to for one and a half days in mid-ocean during a southerly gale after being becalmed for a day off Cape Palliser near Wellington. The crew were warmly welcomed by the Waitangi residents, then after a five-day stay they cleared the Chathams at 5 p.m. on 6 January 1931 to return to Wellington. The weather forecast was for strong to squally north to north-west winds. A shepherd at Ngaio Station on the extreme point of the island watched *Windward* head out into the open sea, until darkness swallowed her.

On 15 January *Windward* was sighted off Cape Palliser by Captain Smith of the motor ship *Enton*. The passage back to Wellington had indeed been slow — *Windward* had averaged only 66 km per day. But when she had not arrived in Wellington a week later the police were advised and all shipping in the area was asked to keep a look-out. Nothing was sighted, and the Prime Minister instructed the master of the Government steamer *Matai* to search the area in which the *Windward* was last seen. Station 2YA Wellington broadcast special instructions on how to change the radio receiver on the Windward into a transmitting set, and a special code distress signal for the crew to transmit was devised. A chain of listening stations made up of amateur ham operators was organised along the entire eastern coastline of New Zealand, but no signals were ever heard.

Day by day the greatest maritime search up to that time was conducted in the whole area of Cook Strait, while the Chatham Islands fishermen searched the ocean around their fishing grounds. In spite of everything possible being done, no trace was ever found of the staunch little *Windward*. It would appear from her last sighting by Captain Smith that she was laying a course for Cape Campbell in the South Island, in a wind from the north-north-west blowing between 28 and 30 knots. No doubt the *Windward's* navigator was hoping for a slant to lay into Wellington Harbour. The wind conditions for the next four days until 19 January continued north-north-west rising to a full gale. It would appear that *Windward* was overwhelmed somewhere in a triangle between Wellington, Cape Palliser and Cape Campbell. Her loss has mystified marine authorities to this day.

No further yacht losses were reported on the New Zealand coast until the Colin Archer-designed, ex-Norwegian pilot cutter *Teddy* was lost on Maori Rock off Kawau Island in the Hauraki Gulf in 1934. Sailed by Norwegian Erling Tambs and his wife and small child, *Teddy* was in the course of a world cruise, having arrived in Auckland in 1930. She was particularly suited for world cruising, measuring 12.2 m overall, 3.9 m in beam with a draught of 2.3 m. Like other Archer designs, she was double-ended with an outboard swung rudder and a low aspect gaff-cutter rig.

She had achieved a great deal of fame during her stay in Auckland. Together with the Australian ketch *Oimara* and the cutter *Rangi* she had taken part in the inaugural trans-Tasman race from Auckland to Sydney. The race started on 14 March 1931. The *Teddy* finished at Sydney on Saturday 28 March, 47 hours behind *Oimara* and six days ahead of *Rangi*, which had experienced navigation problems. On handicap *Teddy* was declared the winner, with *Oimara* second and *Rangi* third.

For this historic win *Teddy* earned herself an enduring place in New Zealand yachting history. Her loss, caused by strong tides sweeping her while becalmed onto Maori Rock, therefore came as a great shock to all New Zealand yachtsmen. Fortunately no lives were lost, but Erling Tambs and his family lost their floating home and all their possessions. A lesson to be learned from the loss of the *Teddy*, which was en route to Sydney with all anchor gear unshackled and stowed, was that until land is well cleared the anchor and necessary lines must be kept on deck ready for use if required.

The next reported incident concerning the loss of yachts off the New Zealand coast was far more serious, and like the missing *Windward* it remains a tragic mystery to this day. This incident involved not one yacht but two, the *Argo* and the *Husky*. There could quite easily have been two more, the *Astral* and the *Aurora*. The circumstances of these losses were somewhat similiar to those involving the *Windward* in the same area exactly 20 years before.

The *Argo* and *Husky* were part of the 20-yacht fleet which started in the Wellington to Lyttelton ocean race in January 1951. This race attracted great interest amongst southern yachtsmen, and was the first of what was to be an annual event organised jointly by the Royal Port Nicholson Yacht Club, the Banks Peninsula Cruising Club and the Akaroa Boating Club.

The 20 yachts entered in the race cleared Wellington Harbour in the early afternoon of 10 January 1951 with a good weather forecast, but in a strange, uneasy easterly. Indeed the fleet had barely entered Palliser Bay before George Brassel, an experienced local fisherman, headed back to Wellington, advising the racing fleet that he did not like the way the weather was looking. At this stage of the race one yacht had already withdrawn; she was the big cutter *Restless*, designed and built by the Tercel brothers in Auckland in 1921. She had been in a collision with the *Argo* at the start and could not continue. The *Argo*, which was designed and built by Percy Voss in Auckland in 1936, broke her bobstay in the collision, but her skipper decided to carry on. It was a fatal decision — she and her crew never returned.

As darkness fell that night, with the fleet spread across Cook Strait, a tremendous southeast gale struck, spreading the stormy conditions over hundreds of square kilometres of ocean. The racing fleet was battered unmercifully and all made for shelter wherever they could. Only one yacht, *Tawhiri* (which had won the 1940 Wellington to Lyttelton centennial race) reached the finish line at Lyttelton; and even then she was disabled and reported missing at one stage.

When the hurricane force winds subsided 36 hours later and the race organisers located what yachts they could, it was found that four were missing. These were the *Astral, Husky, Aurora* and *Argo*.

An immediate search was launched for these four yachts. *Astral* was found in a bad way, dismasted and drifting south of Cape Palliser, by that same George Brassel who had sensed the storm coming and earlier returned to Wellington Harbour. *Astral's* crew, headed by skipper Brian Millar (who in recent years has been very prominent in One-Ton Cup and Admiral's Cup yachts) were uplifted by Brassel's fishing trawler. The *Astral* was left to sink, an inevitable move in her water-logged condition.

The *Aurora* managed to reach shelter at Akaroa and finally made her way to Lyttelton, having retired from the race. She became only the second yacht to arrive at the destination.

This now left two yachts still missing — *Argo* and *Husky*, each with a crew of five men. An immediate air and sea search was commenced, and during the next two days, 13 and 14 January, part of a cabin and other jetsam marked with *Husky's* name were found washed ashore on the southern side of Cook Strait. No trace of *Argo* was found until five days later a solitary life-buoy marked *Argo* was found washed ashore in Palliser Bay. This was to be the only wreckage found from the *Argo*. The vice-commodore of the Royal Port Nicholson Yacht Club at the time, Mr R. J. Campbell, tried valiantly to keep hopes alive when he stated to newspaper reporters that the finding of the life-buoy did not necessarily mean a yacht was lost as he had lost

at least two from his own boat on voyages across Cook Strait.

The air search for the two yachts was discontinued after three days, but after representations by officials of the Royal Port Nicholson Yacht Club to the appropriate authorities, the search was re-started. Special attempts were made to locate the yachts by radio (the same strategy that had been followed during the search for the missing *Windward* 20 years before in the same area). Instructions were transmitted over the national broadcasting system on how to convert an ordinary receiving set into a transmitter. This was relayed very slowly over the national network; earlier, regular transmissions had warned all would-be senders not to use the frequency specified in case they blocked any emergency transmissions, which would be very weak, from the missing yachts.

Messages were received, supposedly from the *Argo*, saying the yacht was dismasted and leaking badly and that the motor was out of action. This meant that the batteries were low and transmissions could not continue for long. Radio fixes on these transmissions showed they originated off the East Cape of the North Island. Intensive sea and air searches were conducted in this area but failed to locate any sign whatsoever of the missing yacht.

Ham radio operators reported hearing similar signals giving the *Argo's* position off the west coast of the southern North Island, but these were regarded as cruel hoaxes. Searching aircraft did cover this area, as it was thought possible that a drifting, dismasted, helpless yacht could be swept by the tides and winds through Cook Strait and into the Tasman Sea.

Hopes of finding the missing yachts faded, and all sea and air searches were called off. What happened to these two well-equipped yachts and their 10 crewmen has remained a mystery to this day.

The radio signals received were never explained. It is possible that the tired, battered crew of *Argo*, working desperately, had managed to convert their radio receiving set into a transmitter, following the instructions broadcast. Their position off the East Cape did not fit into known tide runs off this coast, but the south-east gale which decimated the racing fleet *could* have blown *Argo* into this region. If the radio signals were indeed hoaxes, the cruel mentality of such people cannot be understood.

No radio message was ever received from the

Husky, and it was 15 years before another Wellington to Lyttelton yacht race was held. This was the 1966 race, which was blessed with good weather and 36 entrants — all of which arrived at their destination safely.

The next major incident in New Zealand yachting occurred during the Auckland to Suva ocean race which started on 30 April 1966. A fleet of 37 yachts took part, ranging from the 18.60 m A-class yacht *Fidelis*, owned and skippered by Jim Davern, to the 7.5 m *Clair de Lune*, owned and skippered by P. H. Ensmoore. The oldest yacht in the fleet was the 9.7 m cutter *Kowhai* from Whangarei, sailed by Peter Wilkinson. *Kowhai* had been designed by George Honour as an 8.5 m hard-chined mullet boat. She was later lengthened to 9.7 m overall, with a beam of 2.9 m.

The race started at midday on Saturday 30 April in a moderate to fresh westerly wind. That night the wind lightened, but on Sunday morning it started to blow from the north and soon reached gale force. It stayed this way for the next 48 hours, with the direction varying from north to nor'nor'west. Most of the boats carried on out to sea on the port tack, which took them to the east of the rhumb line. These were considered the right tactics because they would eventually pick up the south-east trades. However the wind lightened and the trade winds did not eventuate.

The northerly gale created havoc with the racing yachts and their crews, who had not yet settled down. There was much seasickness in many boats, some of it serious enough to incapacitate a large percentage of the crew. Two yachts were dismasted. They were the *Huia*, a Herreshoff-designed 11 m ketch sailed by J. R. Hanalon, and *Satanita*, a 13.1 m Sparkman and Stephens design owned and sailed by D. H. R. Wilkie (she was a hot favourite to take handicap honours). Although dismasted, both managed to make their way back to port under jury rig.

Others were forced to retire. They included *Carmen*, a 12.8 m Bob Stewart design sailed by the late Ron Neil, *Fandango*, an 11.6 m Neil Mills-designed sloop sailed by the experienced Ian Titchener (who later owned and sailed the one-tonner *Pathfinder*), *Tamahine O Hau*, a 13.4 m yawl from New Plymouth sailed by E. Persson, and *Horizon* a 10.3 m Woollacott ketch sailed by the Wagstaff brothers. All were forced to retire because of crew seasickness and sail and spar damage.

Many of these yachts were blown off course and ran wildly before the gale, eventually taking shelter in Port Fitzroy, Great Barrier Island, some 320 km south of their position before the gale struck. The severity of the pounding the yachts took can be judged by the fact that two members of *Fandango's* crew suffered broken or cracked ribs, suffered when they were thrown out of their bunks when off watch — in spite of being lashed in.

But the yacht in real trouble was the *Tatariki*, a Woollacott ketch owned and sailed by J. K. Peterson. She measured 10.9 m overall and 9.3 m on the waterline, with a 2.9 beam and a draught of 1.77 m. The *Tatariki* and her seven crew members were a proven and experienced combination, having taken part in the 1964 Whangarei to Noumea race as well as many local offshore races. But what happened could have occurred to any of the yachts in the racing fleet. The gale created unusually confused and very steep seas, with the yachts literally dropping off the crests to slam hard at the bottom.

Then *Tatariki* was hit by a wave which was estimated by one of the crew members to be 13.7 m (45 ft) high. The yacht fell from the crest and hit the bottom of the trough with such force that the garboards round the mast step completely opened up. Within minutes the water inside the yacht was up to the level of the bunks and the crew were baling for their lives.

The water continued to pour in, and it was decided to cut down the mainmast to ease the strain on the open garboards. This drastic action was taken, but the water continued to pour in. In desperation a Mayday call was transmitted at 1334 hours on Monday 2 May 1966.

The call was heard by Auckland Radio, and the Royal New Zealand maritime operations headquarters were immediately advised. So was HMNZS *Endeavour*, which was in the vicinity in her capacity as patrol and communications ship to the racing fleet.

The following is the official log of signals which then followed:

1334 — from *Tatariki*: "Mayday (no position given)."

1335 — from *Endeavour*: "Acknowledge, request position."

1336 — from *Tatariki*: "30 – 40 miles east of North Cape."

1337 — from *Endeavour*: "Check position, which does not agree with earlier D.R. (dead reckoning) positions."

1405 — from *Tatariki*: "Cutting mast away."

1409 — from *Tatariki*: "Can't keep afloat much longer."

1414 — from *Tatariki*: "On last legs. Have steered a northerly course since 0800 position (the regular radio 'sked' when each yacht was required to report their position to the *Endeavour*)."

Nothing further was heard.

An RNZAF Sunderland flying boat was then sent to the position reported by *Tatariki*, and commenced an expanding square search. Two merchant ships, the *Ngakutu* and *Kaitoa*, who were in the area, also started a radar and visual search. Nothing was found, and it appeared that the last position reported by *Tatariki* was grossly incorrect.

RNZAF officers, several of whom were experienced yachtsmen, then started plotting the yacht's possible tracks, based on her 0800 position "sked". They took into account the various reports of wind and sea conditions prevailing in the search area, and deduced the behaviour of the yacht in these conditions — both if sailed hard and high and if eased and riding free. At this time, the Air Force had assumed that *Tatariki* had sunk after her last signal and that they were searching for a 2.4 m dinghy and seven men. A "probability area" was then worked out — a rectangle measuring 62 by 55 nautical miles. In this area, they surmised, lay the *Tatariki* (if she was still afloat) or the dinghy. A check by *Endeavour* of the water temperatures showed that based on survival charts the crew could last only 24 hours if they were in the water.

At nightfall the Sunderland was replaced by a Bristol Freighter, which continued in the "probability area", dropping green flares at regular intervals. The *Endeavour* meanwhile went back to *Tatariki's* reported 0800 position and conducted a random night search from there. The Bristol Freighter reported during that night that it passed over several yachts which shone torches, but the crew were looking for the regulation red flares. They were to learn later that *Tatariki* had jettisoned its red flares accidentally while trying to lighten ship.

With daylight the next day the search was stepped up. A total of seven aircraft were now searching: three Sunderlands, two Dakotas, and a Bristol Freighter in the probability area, with a DC6 covering the area to the west just in case the actual position of the presumed sinking was

between *Tatariki* and the Air Force's estimated position. The *Endeavour* was positioned at the centre of the western end of the probability area to steam at seven knots along the centre line (course 070°) to provide a geographical datum (a reference point) for the searching planes. Two aircraft flew the search on parallel courses 1.60 km apart, giving the lookouts an overlap between the planes. The lookouts were changed at regular intervals, while the radar kept up a constant but rather hopeless sweep in the rough sea conditions.

This search pattern, based on United States Coast Guard practice, was continued all day. Then late in the afternoon a lookout sighted a yacht with a broken mainmast. Those on the plane assumed it was *Huia*, which was not in trouble. The searching planes were looking for a dinghy or survivors in the water, as it was thought *Tatariki* had sunk. However after several low runs the plane positively identified the yacht as the *Tatariki*, and at 1645 hours the *Endeavour* was advised. At 1800 hours *Endeavour* reached the now helpless *Tatariki* and took the crew off. The moderately rough seas were estimated by the naval officers to be between 3.6 m and 7.6 m high, with winds gusting up to 40 knots.

The *Tatariki* was taken in tow at 1815 hours. The tow continued all night, but at daybreak it was seen that *Tatariki* was very low in the water. She was brought alongside to enable a pump to be put aboard, but at 0523 hours (5.23 a.m.) on 8 May *Tatariki* sank. The crew, who lost all their personal possessions, went on to Suva with the *Endeavour*.

So ended the saga of the *Tatariki*. Fortunately, due to the search and rescue services of the Royal New Zealand Air Force and the Royal New Zealand Navy, it did not end with a loss of life. But if it had not been for the prompt, efficient action of these two services *Tatariki* and her seven-man crew would have been lost without trace — as had happened with the *Argo* and *Husky* 15 years before.

The next reported yachting tragedy off the New Zealand coast involved the loss of three generations of the well-known Auckland boatbuilding family, the Lidgards (referred to in a previous chapter), and two crew members, a total of five men. The party was headed by Roy Lidgard, and comprised his son Jim and one of his grandsons, and two young Aucklanders. They were en route to Noumea in a 15.2 m converted oil tender which had been used by the RNZAF to fuel the Sunderland flying boats at Lautoka Bay, Suva. The Lidgards bought this boat and sailed her to Auckland, where they extensively restored her. In early 1968 they sailed from Auckland to salvage a Japanese fishing trawler aground in the New Hebrides. Off North Cape several days later a savage northerly gale was experienced. It must have completely overwhelmed the former oil-tender, which had a very low free-board. In spite of an air search in the area no trace was ever found. The five crew members suffered the same fate as the crews of the *Windward, Argo* and *Husky*.

A rather unusual yachting accident occurred on 14 December 1968. It resulted in the loss of a yacht, but the cool thinking and courage of the skipper and crew and modern lifesaving equipment prevented any loss of life. The yacht was the 12.8 m Spencer-designed *Makatu*, owned by Kemal Lincoln Cox, a Wellington dentist. *Makatu* and her crew of seven experienced yachtsmen left Wellington for Sydney to compete in the 1968 Sydney to Hobart race. She was running before a 30 knot south-wester in longitude 160° east 36° south when she suddenly hit a whale and sank in five minutes. A "mayday" call was transmitted, but the batteries shorted in salt water and the call was never heard. Luckily the sinking was at 1330 hours (1.30 p.m.) so the crew had daylight to abandon ship and put into a swamped, inflatable liferaft. The only provisions they had were four carrots, 14 onions and a 4.5 l tin of methylated spirits. For five days they drifted, to 64 km to the north of the sinking, until they were picked up by the tanker *British Queen*. They quickly recovered on board the tanker, and were taken to Whangarei little the worse for their mishap.

Early in 1970 a trimaran called *Fiddlers Green*, which had been built by Keith McLean, an experienced Auckland yachtbuilder, cleared Auckland for Rarotonga on the first leg of a proposed world cruise. She never arrived and was presumed lost with all hands.

In 1974 an extraordinary little 3.6 m (only 12 ft) yacht named *Sea Egg* arrived in Auckland in the course of a world cruise. She was solo sailed by an English yachtsman, John Riding. He had crossed the Atlantic, and proceeded through the Panama Canal and across the Pacific to New Zealand. The *Sea Egg* remained in Auckland for some months while Riding rested and prepared for a passage across the Tasman to Sydney. Ex-

perienced blue water yachtsmen inspected the little yacht in Auckland and tried to convince Riding not to attempt the Tasman passage. They considered the yacht was not seaworthy. In fact if *Sea Egg* was a New Zealand yacht she would not have been allowed to sail by the Marine Department because she was not equipped with the safety gear required for ocean passages.

Undaunted, Riding ignored all advice and sailed — never to be heard of again. Some days after his departure the northern North Island was lashed by a tropical cyclone, and it is thought *Sea Egg* was sunk in this gale.

Now we come to a loss which is still a mystery. In spite of the most intensive air-sea search, in which thousands of kilometres of ocean were searched and re-searched with the very latest electronic aids, no trace of her was ever found. This yacht was, of course, the 7.3 m ketch *Veronica*.

Veronica was in the course of a delivery voyage to Dunedin when she cleared Gisborne in April 1975. She was crewed by three experienced yachtsmen headed by Tony Hoskyn, an Englishman who had been previously a commander in the Royal Navy and who had sailed extensively not only in New Zealand but all over the world. *Veronica* was fitted with all the necessary equipment for a coastwise passage, including a powerful radio transmitter and receiver. Yet after she cleared Gisborne, no word was ever heard from her. She was never sighted again.

Once it was realised she was missing, a most intensive search was conducted using the Orion aircraft of the RNZAF. These aircraft have radar equipment designed to locate submarines. It is so sensitive that it can locate a kerosene tin 80 km away. Yet radar sweeps were conducted along the whole length of the eastern seaboard of the North Island and 960 km out to sea with no trace being found. After representations to the Government by next of kin and by local yacht clubs, the whole search was repeated with the same result — not a trace of the 7.3 m ketch.

At the time *Veronica* sailed and for some time later the weather was settled, the wind strength moderate and the seas slight. There were certainly no problems for a yacht of her type.

The only possible conclusion that can be drawn from the loss of the *Veronica* is that she suffered the biggest risk all ocean-going yachts face — that of being run down and sunk by a fast-moving freighter steaming at a speed in excess of 20 knots on automatic pilot without lookouts. The *Veronica's* course took her through water fished extensively by large Russian, Japanese and Taiwanese fishing fleets. One of these large trawlers could have run her down, either being unaware of doing so or else never reporting it.

The loss of the *Veronica* is another entry in the chronicle of yachts lost without trace off the New Zealand coast. As the yachting fleets continue to grow in all the main ports it is a regrettable fact that in the future other yachts and crews will be lost. The New Zealand coast is stormy and weather conditions change very rapidly. All yachtsmen contemplating cruising the New Zealand coast should be well equipped with all the necessary safety equipment to reduce the risk of future losses.

14.

The One Ton Cup

NEW ZEALAND'S participation and interest in the One Top Cup competition dates back to 1968 when Chris Bouzaid went to a yachting centre in the North Sea called Heligoland, a place most New Zealand yachtsmen had never heard of up to that time. Yet although the One Ton Cup was new in this country, in 1968 it had been competed for since 1899 by European countries.

This elaborate, ornate and rather overdressed creation of finely-worked water-lily leaves was carved by a French goldsmith called Linzeler from a 10 kg block of solid silver for several club members of the Cercle de la Voile de Paris. They had just sold their shares in the 20 tonne ocean racer *Esterel*, which had been built to defend the Coupe de France in Cannes in 1898. These members stipulated that the La Coupe Internationale du Cercle de La Voile de Paris (the full and correct name of the One Ton Cup) be raced for by yachts matching up to the then one-ton class rule. The Cercle de la Voile de Paris received the trophy most enthusiastically, for this was the first major international trophy to be competed for by such a small class.

The first challenge was held in 1899 at Meulan on the River Seine, when the French yacht *Belouga*, sailed by Eugene Laverne and the Michelot brothers, beat the English challenger *Vectis*, representing the Island Sailing Club. Anglo-French competition continued for the next five challenges from 1900 to 1906 (there were no races in 1903 and 1904), France winning three and England two.

To attract more international entries, it was decided in 1907 to discontinue the one-ton class

as such. The first international rating rules were now drawn up for the international 6 m class, and the One Ton Cup was assigned to this new class. This move proved very successful. Five countries — Germany, England, France, Belgium and Spain — entered yachts. An entry from the German club Norddeutscher Regatta Verein won the trophy, and for the next two challenges defended it. In 1910 the Swedish entry *Agnes II*, competing for the first time, beat the Germans and began the Scandinavian domination of the One Ton Cup which reached its peak from 1929 to 1952. Not until the early 1950s was an American yacht *Llanoria*, able to take the trophy. In the 1953 contest held in Long Island Sound off New York the Swiss yacht *Ylliam VIII* won the cup back for the Europeans. Then in 1957 the hardy American *Llanoria* again broke the European domination.

It was becoming obvious that the international 6 m class was on the way out, and in 1962 competition for the One Ton Cup was discontinued. In 1930 eight countries had challenged for the cup, held that year in Stockholm, but in 1961 and 1962 only Sweden, Switzerland and England challenged the current holder, France. It was fitting that the French, who started the competition, should hold the cup at the time it was decided to discontinue the series.

Since the inception of the One Ton Cup in 1899 Sweden had won the trophy 13 times, England 12, France nine, Norway five, Germany and Switzerland four each, and Holland and the United States two each.

The trophy was uncontested in 1963 and 1964. Like so many yachting trophies it appeared to be heading for oblivion, until the commodore of the Cercle de la Voile de Paris, Jean Peytel, began campaigning for its revival under a new rating rule. He consulted the leading British designer and yachtsman at the time, John Illingworth, for his opinion of what class of yacht the revamped competition would best suit.

Left: This yacht has perhaps had more influence on New Zealand yachting than any other. Chris Bouzaid on the helm of the Sparkman and Stephens-designed *Rainbow II* coaxes all the speed he can from her, while the crew lie out on the windward deck. A photograph taken during the 1969 One Ton Cup contest off Heligoland, which she won.

After due consideration Illingworth replied that he felt that a series of one-rating races under the R.O.R.C. (Royal Ocean Racing Club) limit of 6.7 m (22 ft) would be the ideal competition, but he thought the rules regarding cabin fittings and the like should be tightened. He also stated that continual revising of the regulations would need to be carried out in the future if useful boats were to survive the intense competition (that is to say, preserve their ability to be practical and durable fast cruisers). Prophetic words indeed — some of the "throw-aways" now being designed to take advantage of rule discrepancies are proof that Illingworth's concern nearly 15 years ago is today being realised.

The new rating for the One Ton Cup was received with great enthusiasm, and at the 1965 contest held at Le Havre 14 yachts from eight countries competed. The great designers of the world were represented, and the Sparkman and Stephens-designed *Diana III* won for Denmark. At Copenhagen in 1966 the number of challengers had risen to 24, from nine countries. It was becoming obvious that the world's leading designers were using the One Ton Cup contest as a testing ground for radical advances in hull form and construction. Sailmakers were realising the promotional benefit of having their sails and material used by the winner and they began to take a close interest.

The 1966 challenge, sailed in very calm conditions, was won by the beamy 7.32 m American *Tina*, designed by the relatively unknown Dick Carter. *Tina* was based on his first R.O.R.C. design *Rabbit*, which sensationally won the 1965 Fastnet Race after being disqualified in the Harwich Hook race, in which she finished first because the pulpit did not meet R.O.R.C. specifications. The 1967 contest was held at Le Havre, and 21 yachts from 10 countries competed. This time Carter was again successful, with *Optimist* from Germany, a development of the *Tina* design.

In 1968 New Zealand participated for the first time. The yacht was called *Rainbow II*, representing the Royal New Zealand Yacht Squadron. She was skippered by a young man named Chris Bouzaid and his crew of almost fanatical Kiwis managed by Arnold Baldwin. After a tense series of races *Rainbow II* was beaten by the German yacht *Optimist*, brilliantly sailed by sailmaker Hans Beilken. From the five races in the series Bielken achieved the tally of first-second-first-first-first for a total of 116 and a half

points. Chris Bouzaid in *Rainbow II* managed a tally of third-sixth-second-third-third for 107 points and second, while the Italian entry *Kerkyra* took third place with 101 and a quarter points from a tally of second-first-fourth-eighth-thirteenth.

It was New Zealand's pioneering venture in international rating class racing. Chris Bouzaid and his crew returned home with a lot of lessons learnt about this type of racing and with a quiet determination to return to Europe for the next series and to win the coveted One Ton Cup.

Back in New Zealand the success of *Rainbow II* had created great interest in the one-ton class of yacht. Yachts in this class were 11-11.5 m overall, with tremendous beam and a moderate sail area. They would be well suited to racing and also family cruising in the Hauraki Gulf. The 1969 season saw the launching of 14 keelers matching the One Ton Cup specifications, including *Rebel* (Brin Wilson), *Rogue* (John Senior, who later owned the Bruce Farr-designed Admiral's Cup trialist *Kailua*), *Renegade* (John Lidgard) and *Panther* (Ian Lichenstein). All were keen to compete against and hopefully beat the second-best one-tonner in the world, *Rainbow II*.

If ever a yacht revolutionized yachting in New Zealand it was *Rainbow II*. She was the first displacement-type fin keeler built in this country, but she was not the first Sparkman and Stephens racing design built here; that honour goes to Peter Spencer's *Cotton Blossom IV*, built by Max Carter in 1960. Two other Sparkman and Stephens designs — Ron Wilkie's *Satanita* and the Yates cousins' *Jupiter* — had also predated *Rainbow II*.

During the 1967 New Zealand yachting season — before her 1968 One Ton Cup success — *Rainbow II* had shown remarkable speed. Her record in that season was outstanding. She won her first race — a Royal New Zealand Yacht Squadron round-the-island race of 56 km — 24 hours after she was launched. Two weeks later she started in the Whangarei to Noumea race and averaged over seven knots for the 1600 km, beating *Fidelis* to win the race by one and a half hours on corrected time. She made the New Zealand Southern Cross team for 1967, New Zealand being just beaten by New South Wales. Then she won the famous Sydney to Hobart ocean race, the last of the series on corrected time in gale conditions from the French entry *Pen Duick*.

So *Rainbow II* and her crew had certainly proved their ability before the 1968 One Ton Cup contest at Heligoland. Now their second placing made them more determined to win the 1969 series, again to be sailed on the waters of Heligoland. It was a tricky sailing area of strong tides and contrary light winds, which Bouzaid and his navigator Alan Warwick were now familar with.

But two things had to be done. Firstly she had to be made more competitive, with a bigger sail area, if she was to beat *Optimist* in the light conditions. To keep within the rating *Rainbow II* needed heavier scantlings. This was achieved by fitting a heavier deck and installing a larger and heavier engine. These modifications allowed 990 mm to be added to the mast height. *Rainbow II* now had a sail area only slightly less than *Optimist*. The second factor that remained was that *Rainbow II* still needed to qualify to represent New Zealand, and the competition from the ever increasing fleet of competitive one-ton class yachts in Auckland was going to be tough.

Rainbow II was rigged for the light German conditions for the New Zealand qualifying trials, which were held at Easter, at a time when winds are traditionally strong, over four races — one offshore and three over 48 km Olympic course events. In the first race, the offshore event, *Rainbow II* carried away her rudder and had to retire. But she won the next three and thus also the right to represent New Zealand.

Again the Royal New Zealand Yacht Squadron sponsored the challenge, and *Rainbow II* worked up to the one-ton series by competing at the week-long Keil Regata. In light wind conditions she won on corrected times every race that she entered.

But the contest off Heligoland was the big event. *Rainbow II* won the first race by three minutes and the second by two and a half minutes. The third race was the long ocean event, and conditions varied from flat calm to 30 knots. After a tense gybing duel with arch rival *Optimist* in the last leg, *Rainbow II* went on to win by nine minutes. The fourth race, a short event, was again won by *Rainbow II* after a very tight tacking contest with *Optimist*. Bouzaid had won four of the five races, and the One Ton Cup was going south of the Equator for the first time — to far-distant New Zealand.

Rainbow II never returned to New Zealand. She was sold to a yachtsman in Bermuda, and as far as is known is still sailing in Bermudian

The Sparkman and Stephens-designed one-tonner *Young Nick*, owned by Lou Fisher, but sailed by Alan Warwick, runs very comfortably "downhill" during the One Ton Cup series off Auckland in 1971.

waters. If ever a yacht should have been preserved for the future — like Sir Francis Chichester's *Gypsy Moth* — it should have been *Rainbow II*.

The 1971 One Ton Cup contest was to be held in Auckland, and the organisation responsible for the event was the host club, the Royal New Zealand Yacht Squadron. This was most appropriate because this senior club of New Zealand yachting was to celebrate its centenary in that year.

There had been sweeping changes in the rating adopted for the One Ton Cup contest. The R.O.R.C. limit of 6.7 m was dropped and replaced by the 8.4 m I.O.R. (International Offshore Rating) MK II limit. Many top yachtsmen and officials consider that this rating (which was set at 8.4 m to keep the R.O.R.C. boats in the class) was a serious mistake. The new I.O.R.-designed yachts were now allowed to become very large and consequently very expensive. If the rating had been fixed at around 7.5 m their cost would have been less. There would be more boats and therefore more interest. The very recent upsurge in the number of quarter and half-ton rating yachts at the expense of the one-tonners bears this criticism out.

With the 1971 One Ton Cup contest being held in Auckland, a tremendous spate of yacht building began. The first of the new yachts built to the I.O.R. 8.4 m rating was the Sparkman and

Stephens Swan 37 *Young Nick*, built for Mr Lou Fisher; she was to be sailed by Alan Warwick. Gil Hedges, who had previously sailed the steel half-tonner *Interlude*, then announced he would have a sister ship, *Escapade*, built in aluminium alloy by Steel Yachts and Launches Ltd and commissioned for the trials to select the New Zealand team. At the same time Ted Buchanan of Whangarei announced that he too would build a wooden Swan 37, to be called *Kishmul*. John Lidgard entered the fray with his *Runaway*. Keith Henley commissioned Hal Wagstaff to design *Skinflint*, and Noel Angus embarked on a crash programme to get a Cuthbert and Cassian design, *Mustang*, into the water in time for the trials.

The man who made the Auckland contest possible did not yet have a boat and was at this

A classic photograph of *Outrage*, owned by Clyde Colson of Whangarei, here during the 1971 One Ton Cup trials. The crew line the windward decks, while the skipper and winch-hand utilise every lift possible.

Great photographs of New Zealand one-tonners in action during the One Ton Cup trials off Auckland in 1971. *Runaway* and *Concord* to windward, with *Escapade* just pushing her bow into the picture, slog in fresh conditions. Lower left: *Concord* (265) and *Escapade* are hard on the wind in light airs. Lower right: the yachts duel for position at race start. *Young Nick* runs for the line, while to leeward *Outrage* (268) and *Wai-Aniwa* take similar action.

stage only an interested spectator. Chris Bouzaid was worried that all these Sparkman and Stephens designs would not prove a match for the Dick Carter-designed *Optimist B* that his arch rival Hans Beilken was bringing to Auckland. Ray Walker, a wealthy Auckland industrialist, also realised this possibility and had a Carter-designed near-sister to *Optimist B* built from aluminium. He called her *Wai-Aniwa*, and Bouzaid was offered the helm.

The trial series was as competitive as the actual cup contest. History now records that the New Zealand team comprised *Young Nick, Escapade* and only just *Wai-Aniwa*, which just pipped an unknown yacht called *Moonlight* sailed by Peter Mulgrew for the third position.

The 1971 One Ton Cup contest attracted a bigger entry than the previous contest at Heligoland. There were nine countries and 17 yachts, a tribute to the organisation of the Royal New Zealand Yacht Squadron. All the top designers were represented, and the hot favourites were the Italian entry *Kerkya IV* (the latest Sparkman and Stephens creation sailed by Rear Admiral Agostino Straulino and owned by Mrs Marina Spaccarelli Bulgari), *Optimist B* (designed by Dick Carter and sailed by Hans Beilken) and *Wai-Aniwa*.

No-one paid much attention to an Australian entry called *Stormy Petrel*, a G.R.P. Swan 37 owned and sailed by a shrewd tactician named Syd Fischer with a hard-driving crew of Sydney "eighteens" men. *Stormy Petrel* was a "character" yacht, having a stock fibreglass coach roof moulding from a Swanson 36 fitted to the Swan 37 hull, which did nothing for her looks. She had taken a battering in the 1970 Sydney to Hobart race, and it was rumoured that the decking was coming away from the hull. In fact one of her crew made the classic remark after the series that her topsides were watertight — it was only the deck and hull that leaked.

But when it was all over *Stormy Petrel* had a five-race tally of first-first-sixth-first-sixth and 89 and five-eights points. She was a clear winner from *Optimist B* with a tally of sixth-fifth-first-eighth-first and 74 points, with *Young Nick* third with 72 points. The glamour yachts, *Wai-Aniwa* and *Kerkyra IV*, did not relish the light conditions experienced through the contest and finished a disappointing fifth and eighth respectively.

There was one consolation for the New Zealand yachtsmen. The Australian win meant that the 1972 contest would be held just across the Tasman in Sydney. It would have been held back in Europe if New Zealand had won, as the rules state that every second defence by a non-European country must be held in European waters (to prevent the America's Cup situation where the holder has the distinct advantage of always sailing in home waters.)

The *Kerkyra IV* had failed to win the cup, but her patches of brilliance impressed the canny, experienced Auckland boatbuilder Brin Wilson. He built a sister ship, which he called *Pathfinder*, and the wisdom of this decision was soon apparent. In October 1971 the Royal Akarana Yacht Club ran trials for that year's Southern Cross Cup team, which proved to be the one-tonners *Pathfinder, Runaway* and *Wai-Aniwa*. This team performed only moderately well in the short races on Sydney Harbour, but in the 1971 Sydney to Hobart race produced the famous first, second, third victory (*Pathfinder, Runaway, Wai-Aniwa*) for New Zealand. The Southern Cross Cup was in New Zealand for two years.

The 1972 One Ton Cup contest in Sydney attracted great interest in Auckland, but no new boats. The New Zealand team consisted of *Young Nick* (sailed by Alan Warwick), *Pathfinder* (sailed for new owner Ian Titchener by Roy Dickson) and *Wai-Aniwa* (sailed by Chris Bouzaid). After a rather uninspiring series not helped by the crack German entry *Ydra* (sailed by Hans Beilken) losing her forestay and therefore all chances of winning in the high-scoring ocean race, Chris Bouzaid won the One Ton Cup for the Royal New Zealand Yacht Squadron. He displayed consistent sailing, aided by luck in the last race.

The Carter-designed *Ydra* looked the yacht to beat in the 1973 contest, which was to be held in Porto Cervo, Italy, only eight months after the Sydney series. No new New Zealand one-tonners had been built since *Pathfinder*, and the R.N.Z.Y.S. decided to charter a fibreglass stock version of the Carter design, called *Hann*, for Bouzaid and his crew. But the *Hann* could not be properly tuned and was not competitive, and the cup went to the *Ydra* (this time sailing for Italy under sailing master Admiral Straulino). The American yacht *Ganbare*, designed by newcomer Doug Peterson and with New Zealander Ron Holland in the crew, proved a real flier and was unlucky not to win.

This yacht impressed Chris Bouzaid so much that in partnership with one of his crew members, Bevan Woolley, he had a sister ship built on his return to Auckland by boatbuilder Tim Gurr. She was built from foam sandwich, and was called *Streaker*. This yacht has never sailed to her potential in spite of extensive modifications, and is today shaded by the latest designs from Bruce Farr.

The 1974 one-ton contest was held at Torbay in England, where Bouzaid and his crew sailed a chartered yacht of the *Ganbare* design. They finished a creditable third behind the British-owned and sailed and Peterson-designed *Gumboots*. New Zealand took a breather in the 1975 contest held at Newport, United States, where the cup was won for the first time since the I.O.R. 8.4 m rule was adopted in 1970 by an American yacht. She was *Pied Piper*, designed by Doug Peterson and sailed by Ted Turner.

The 1976 contest at Marseilles, France, was again the scene of an all-out New Zealand at-

Another shot from the 1971 trials. Chris Bouzaid on the port tack sails *Wai-Aniwa* into the Tiri Passage while *Escapade* and *Moonlight* continue on the starboard tack.

tempt to win the cup, this time with the Bruce Farr-designed *45 South* (formerly *The Number*) sailed by Graeme Woodroffe, and *Jiminy Cricket*, sailed by Stuart Brentnall, whose crew included Chris Bouzaid.

The New Zealand team were keen to win the cup, as the 1977 contest was to be held off Auckland in the waters of the Hauraki Gulf.

The New Zealand trials were contested by a top-class field of all the competitive New Zealand one-tonners. There was the *Streaker*, sailed by the very experienced Chris Bouzaid and her co-owner Bevan Woolley, who had sailed on the *Rainbow II* with Bouzaid. There was *Checkmate*, a radical design from Jim Young and sailed by him, and a whole host of Farr-designed one-tonners headed by *Mardi Gras*, sailed by Chris Beckett, and *Rockie*, sailed by Peter Kingston (who was later to be appointed manager of the New Zealand team). Notably missing from the trials were the Sparkman and Stephens designs which had dominat-

The shape of a fine one-tonner and champion ocean racer. *Pathfinder* in the Lyttelton dry dock in 1974 after racing from Auckland.

ed the New Zealand One Ton Cup fleets in previous years. These heavy displacement designs had proved no match for the ultra light displacement Farr creations and had dropped out of the One Ton Cup scene.

After a most exciting home trial series *The Number*, just beat *Jiminy Cricket*, but the result could have gone to either boat. These two yachts completely dominated the fleet, although at times both *Rockie* and *Mardi Gras* looked good, and *Checkmate* promised potential speed when properly tuned.

Public interest was high and it was strongly suggested that both *The Number* and *Jiminy Cricket* be sent to Marseilles instead of only the winner as originally intended. The yacht club that organised the trials and the New Zealand challenge, the Royal New Zealand Yacht Squadron, now appealed to the public for funds to also send the runner-up, *Jiminy Cricket*. Owner Stuart Brentnall assisted financially and it was decided to send a two-boat team. In the meantime *The Number* had been renamed *45° South*.

The 1976 One Ton Cup contest was notable for the 20 yacht designers represented. The American Doug Peterson was the most prolific, with 13 yachts of his design racing; Bruce Farr had four yachts, the two from New Zealand, one from England and one from Italy. These latter two were the latest from his drawing board — they were the "light air designs", slightly smaller in hull size with more sail, carrying 83 sq m spinnakers and 32 sq m genoas. Ron Holland also had four designs; they had huge rigs with 140 sq m spinnakers and 66 sq m genoas. American Scott Kaufman had two, with fellow-countrymen Britton Chance and Gary Mull one each.

There were two very notable absentees — Sparkman and Stephens and Dick Carter, whose designs had previously dominated all One Ton Cup contests. The last win Sparkman and Stephens had enjoyed was in 1971 with *Stormy Petrel*, Carter in 1973 with *Ydra*. This really demonstrates how in this very tough level of competition designers must keep up with all the latest trends in design as well as construction techniques. New Zealand-domiciled designers such as Bruce Farr and Paul Whiting, so far from the mainstream of Northern hemisphere developments, must find it very difficult to keep abreast of design and construction techniques.

Many of the big names in world yachting were participating in the 1976 contest. Ted Turner

Chris Bouzaid and Bevan Woolley's one-tonner *Streaker*, here reaching at speed.

and Lowell North were there as cup defenders in *Pied Piper*. Britton Chance was co-helming *Resolute Salmon* with Dick Deaver, who had just won the Congressional Cup in California. Butch Dalrymple-Smith, who sailed on *Stormy Petrel* in 1971, was sailing the Spanish entry *Silver Apple*. Hans Beilken was sailing the German yacht *Caliqu VIII*, and the Englishman Jeremy Rodgers, who had sailed the 1974 winner *Gumboots*, was sailing *Karate* for Britain. The American designer Scott Kaufman was on board his own design *America Jane III*.

The New Zealand entries did not relish the light wind conditions, which at their strongest over the five races barely exceeded 20 knots. Yet there seemed to be a distinct chance of the cup coming to New Zealand for the third time when *45 South* won the 43 km first race, with *Jiminy Cricket* second. In the second race, subsequently resailed because the first mark was out of position, *Jiminy Cricket* finished fifth, with *45 South* eighth. The third race was of 257 km; *45 South* was eighth and *Jiminy Cricket* ninth. The resailed second race (sailed immediately after the third race) proved a complete disaster for the

Jiminy Cricket, which so nearly won the 1976 One Ton Cup.

The Number, renamed *45 South*, rounds a mark during the 1976 One Ton Cup series off the French coast.

New Zealand yachts, *45 South* finishing ninth and *Jiminy Cricket*, not handling the wind shifts, finishing an unbelievable forty-first.

Race four, a 48 km triangular course, was won by *45 South* with *Jiminy Cricket* second. At this stage *Resolute Salmon* had a clear overall lead, with *America Jane* second, *Pied Piper* third and *45 South* fourth. *Jiminy Cricket* was ninth overall. The ocean race proved a triumph for *Jiminy Cricket*, who won it from *Natael III* of Italy and *Canquien* of France. *45 South* finished in eighteenth position just behind *Re-* *solute Salmon* and *Pied Piper*. *Jiminy Cricket* would have won the One Ton Cup by a huge margin if that controversial second race had not been resailed, or if she had finished better than that disastrous forty-first position. In this type of racing consistency is the keynote; *Resolute Salmon*, with consistent sailing, proved a worthy winner.

It is appropriate here to record the past winners of the One Ton Cup since its inception in France in 1899:

YEAR	PLACE	WINNER	COUNTRY	CLASS
1898	Meulan	*Belouga*	France	one-ton
1900	Meulan	*Sidi Fekkar*	France	one-ton
1901	Meulan	*Scotia II*	Britain	one-ton
1902	Cowes	*Scotia III*	Britain	one-ton
1903	Cowes	*Chocolat*	France	one-ton
1904-5		Not competed for		
1906	Meulan	*Feu Follet*	France	one-ton
1907	Meulan	*Onkel Adolph*	Germany	6 m
1908	Kiel	*Windspiel XI*	Germany	6 m
1909	Kiel	*Windspiel XII*	Germany	6 m
1910	Kiel	*Agnes II*	Sweden	6 m
1911	Goteborg	*Windspiel XV*	Germany	6 m
1912	Kiel	*Bunty*	Britain	6 m
1913	Cowes	*Cremona*	Britain	6 m
1914-19		Not competed for		
1920	Cowes	*Cordella*	Britain	6 m
1921	Ryde	*Cordella*	Britain	6 m
1922	Ryde	*Cordella*	Britain	6 m
1923	Ryde	*Cordella*	Britain	6 m
1924	Ryde	*Holland's Hope*	Holland	6 m
1925	Amsterdam	*Princess Juliana*	Holland	6 m
1926	Amsterdam	*Zenith*	Britain	6 m
1927	Ryde	*Petite Aile II*	France	6 m
1928	Meulan	*Yara III*	France	6 m
1929	Deauville	*Bissbi*	Sweden	6 m
1930	Stockholm	*Bissbi*	Sweden	6 m
1931	Stockholm	*Bissbi*	Sweden	6 m
1932	Stockholm	*Abu*	Norway	6 m
1933	Oslo	*Varg V*	Norway	6 m
1934	Oslo	*White Lady*	Norway	6 m
1935	Oslo	*Jan III*	Sweden	6 m
1936	Goteborg	*Tidsfordrif*	Sweden	6 m
1937	Goteborg	*Tidsfordrif II*	Sweden	6 m
1938	Goteborg	*Norna VI*	Norway	6 m
1939	Oslo	*Noreg III*	Norway	6 m

YEAR	PLACE	WINNER	COUNTRY	CLASS
1940-45		Not competed for		
1946	Oslo	*May Be VI*	Sweden	6 m
1947	Stockholm	*May Be VI*	Sweden	6 m
1948	Goteborg	*May Be VI*	Sweden	6 m
1949	Stockholm	*Trickson VI*	Sweden	6 m
1950	Stockholm	*May Be VI*	Sweden	6 m
1951		Not competed for		
1952	Stockholm	*Lianoria*	U.S.	6 m
1953	Long Island	*Ylliam VIII*	Switzerland	6 m
1954	Geneva	*Ylliam IX*	Switzerland	6 m
1955	Stockholm	*Ylliam IX*	Switzerland	6 m
1956	Cannes	*Ylliam IX*	Switzerland	6 m
1957	Oslo	*Lianoria*	U.S.	6 m
1958	Le Havre	*Royal Thames*	Britain	6 m
1959	Poole Bay	*May Be VIII*	Sweden	6 m
1960	Goteborg	*Elghi III*	France	6 m
1961	Cannes	*Elghi III*	France	6 m
1962	Palma de Mallorca	*Elghi III*	France	6 m
1963-64		Not competed for		
1965	Le Havre	*Diana III*	Denmark	7.7 m R.O.R.C.
1966	Copenhagen	*Tina*	U.S.	7.7 m R.O.R.C.
1967	Le Havre	*Optimist*	Germany	7.7 m R.O.R.C.
1968	Heligoland	*Optimist*	Germany	7.7 m R.O.R.C.
1969	Heligoland	*Rainbow II*	New Zealand	7.7 m R.O.R.C.
1970		Not competed for		
1971	Auckland	*Stormy Petrel*	Australia	8.4m I.O.R. MkII
1972	Sydney	*Wai-Aniwa*	New Zealand	8.4m I.O.R. MkII
1973	Porto Cervo	*Ydra*	Italy	8.4m I.O.R. MkII
1974	Torbay	*Gumboots*	Britain	8.4m I.O.R. MkII
1975	Newport	*Pied Piper*	U.S.	8.4m I.O.R. MkII
1976	Marseilles	*Resolute Salmon*	U.S.	8.4m I.O.R. MkII

15.

Ocean racing in New Zealand

THE RACING OF YACHTS across the oceans of the world has been likened to standing under a cold shower ripping up $10 notes — a wet, cold, expensive game. Yet each year more and more yachts are entered in ocean races, ranging from the older-style heavy displacement boats to the modern, ultra-light I.O.R. racing machines. They are built from a variety of materials, ranging from the traditional wood through ferro-cement to fibreglass and aluminium — and in the future, laminations of glass reinforced with carbon fibre and stressed with alloy tubing.

In spite of all possible safety precautions ocean racing will always be a dangerous sport. Like mountaineering, it pits man against the elements. Perhaps this is the attraction — the element of danger which provides the challenge. That is certainly something which has been removed from our modern way of life.

Whatever the stimulus, ocean racing is very popular. Look at the 130 entries in the 1977 Auckland to Suva yacht race — the largest fleet ever to assemble in New Zealand for an ocean race. So large was this fleet that in the interests of safety, the organisers (the Royal Akarana Yacht Club) were forced to split the fleet into two divisions. In category one the racing yachts, basically the rating classes, sailed to Suva, while the cruising boats in category two raced to Lautoka. Compare this situation with the 16 yachts which sailed in the inaugural Auckland to Suva ocean race in 1956.

Ocean racing in New Zealand is a comparatively new sport. It owes its origins to an Australian yachtsman, Frank Bennell of the Royal St. Kilda Yacht Club in Melbourne. Mr Bennell owned the ketch *Oimara* which measured 12.8 m overall, 3.2 m beam with a draught of 2.9 m. She was unusual in that she carried a squaresail yard on her mainmast. Bennell was fired with the ambition to race across the Tasman, either east to west or west to east. He issued challenges in Australia, without attracting much

interest, so decided to sail *Oimara* to New Zealand to challenge New Zealand yachtsmen. In December 1930 he sailed to Wellington, carrying a fully certified wireless operator who used the same radio equipment which Sir Charles Kingsford Smith had used in his historic first-ever flight across the Tasman two years earlier. Arriving in Wellington, he found there was no interest in his challenge, so he proceeded on to Auckland. Here the challenge was accepted by Erling Tambs in his Norwegian pilot cutter *Teddy*. (We have already discussed the total loss of this fine vessel in chapter 13.)

Bennell and Tambs agreed that the race would start on Saturday 14 March 1931. In spite of strenuous efforts to attract other yachts, it appeared that only the *Oimara* and *Teddy* would start. It came as a surprise therefore when only six days before the race was scheduled to start Mr Allan Leonard entered the race with his gaff-rigged cutter *Rangi*. *Rangi* had been built in 1902 by Bailey and Lowe at Auckland. She measured 9.3 m overall, 3.2 m in beam and had a draft of 1.7 m. She was launched as the *Schopolo* and had been used as a fishing vessel for 14 years before being converted into a pleasure yacht.

Rangi had proved a fast yacht in local competitions over the years, and was now considered by local yachtsmen to be the favourite to win the trans-Tasman race. But the very short notice posed problems in preparing her. She was essentially a gulf and harbour racer, but this was to be very much a "deep sea" passage. Her crew working feverishly against time, she was slipped and anti-fouled, and the small auxilary motor she was fitted with was removed and the shaft log plugged. The large open cockpit was partially enclosed, and extra sails and gear as well as the necessary provisions for the race were loaded aboard. In fact it was not until 30 minutes after the other two competitors *Teddy* and *Oimara* had started at 2 p.m. that *Rangi* actually floated off the grid in St. Mary's Bay and made

Left: The thrill and sheer power of ocean racing as *Pathfinder* slams into a big sea. Note the I.O.R. safety measures. On deck is the self-inflatable six-man life raft. The sea rails for'ard are all reinforced with lashing to prevent crewmen being washed through them. Both deck and halyard winches can be seen, while the slab reefing system along the boom shows the efficiency of the modern ocean racing yacht.

A sister ship to the *Rangi*. The Auckland snapper fishing cutter *Skobeloff*, built by Bailey and Lowe a year after *Rangi*, in 1903.

her way down to the start-line off King's Wharf.

The day was brilliantly fine with a light south-west breeze. The largest fleet of pleasure boats ever seen up to that time escorted the racing yachts past North Head and into the Rangitoto Channel. The crews of the three yachts were as follows:

Oimara: F. J. Bennell (skipper), J. Bennell (son of the owner), C. Constance of Auckland and Captain H. C. Symonds (navigator).

Teddy: E. Tambs (skipper and navigator) and four Aucklanders — R. Goodwin, E. W. Bone, H. Brown and W. J. Parkinson.

Rangi: Lt. Com. W. C. Juler, late Royal Australian Navy (skipper and navigator), and Aucklanders D. Kirkcaldie, A. Clark and E. Spraggon.

The *Oimara* carried the number 59 on the peak of her mainsail, the *Teddy* No.1 on her mainsail. The *Rangi* had her Auckland registration number B. 16 on her mainsail.

No trophies or prize money had been organised between the yachts, so it came as a surprise when the Akarana Yacht Club (it did not receive the Royal charter until 1938) presented a silver cup 24 hours before the start which was inscribed: *Trans-Tasman Cup. Inaugurated March 1931, presented by the Akarana Yacht Club, Auckland, New Zealand.*

At a meeting of the crews the day before the race the following handicaps were declared: *Oimara*, scratch; *Rangi*, 73 and a half hours; and *Teddy*, 96 hours.

The yachts carried the south-west breeze up the eastern coast of the North Island to North Cape, where *Oimara* held a handy lead. This lead had been helped by the use of her auxiliary motor in calm periods (this was later admitted by her skipper, but the other competitors did not ask for a disqualification. Perhaps it may have been different if *Oimara* had won the trophy.)

Forty-eight hours after rounding North Cape, *Oimara* was struck by gale-force winds from the south with associated heavy seas. In the evening

of 21 March a severe squall broke the mainsail gaff and blew out the mainsail and jib. Skipper Frank Bennell, who was at the wheel, was thrown against the mizzen mast and suffered a broken nose. Fortunately, crew members were able to push it into shape and strap it up. The rest of the race was uneventful for *Oimara* . She was first yacht to arrive at Sydney — at 10.40 a.m. on 26 March 1931, after a passage of 11 days and 20 hours.

Teddy cleared North Cape on 16 March and picked up a fresh south-westerly, which she carried for two days under mainsail and spinnaker, at times logging nine and a half knots. But she ran into calms, and for the next five days barely moved. She then picked up a fresh south-easterly, arriving at the finish-line at noon on Saturday 28 March.

Rangi did not finish until 5 a.m. on 3 April, after a passage of 19 days and 16 hours. It was a voyage plagued with stormy conditions and faulty navigation equipment. In fact she was 386 km off course when they sighted Green Cape on the southern New South Wales coast, having to then sail north to Sydney Heads.

This first race attracted a great deal of attention on both sides of the Tasman; ocean racing had arrived in the Southern Hemisphere.

There had, of course, been other non-racing Tasman passages, all from New Zealand to Australia and all being delivery voyages from Auckland boatbuilders to Australian owners. The vessels were sailed by professional seamen.

The first of these passages was by the yacht *Secret* in 1875. *Taniwha*, a 29-tonner built by George Niccol at Devonport, was sailed to Melbourne on 4 December 1880, arriving 10 days later. *Waitangi*, a straight-stemmer built for Mr A. Newton of Melbourne, was sailed to her new owner in 1878 by Captain J. Hardy and crew. The Logan brothers cutter *Rawhiti*, owned by Mr A. T. Pittar, was sailed to Sydney from Auckland in 1905 under trysail rig by a crew of five when her owner emigrated to Australia. (*Rawhiti* returned to Auckland in 1946.) The cutter *Rainbow* also sailed to Sydney to compete against Australian yachts.

The first recorded passage to the Pacific Islands by a yacht was by the Charles Bailey Junior-built cutter *Koe Fetuue Aho* ("the morning star") in 1912. Bailey built the yacht for the Free Church of Tonga, and she measured 13.7 m overall, 4.2 m in beam, and drew 1.7 m. She was gaff cutter-rigged. Sailed by Captain Stenbeck and a crew of two, *Koe Fetuue Aho* left Auckland on 25 June 1912 and dropped anchor off the Nuku'alofa wharf on 4 July, a passage of 2107 km in nine days. Captain Stenbeck, a Norwegian by birth, also sailed the *Onelua* (a 15.8 m cutter designed and built by Charles Bailey Junior for the King of Tonga) to Tonga in 1917. This fine cutter, which was wrecked in 1921, sailed the 1771 km to Tonga in seven days under just trysail and staysail. Captain Stenbeck was drowned off the Coromandel Coast in May 1937 while sailing his ketch *Yvonne*.

However the first ocean passage by amateur yachtsmen was the cruise of the cutter *Victory*, owned by Auckland yachtsman Harold George to Norfolk Island and return in 1928. Like the *Rangi*, *Victory* was built originally as a fishing boat. Built by the Logan brothers in 1906, she measured 11.6 m overall, 8.5 m on the waterline, 2.8 m in beam, with a draught of 1.8 m. She was gaff cutter-rigged. She cleared Auckland on 19 December 1928 with a crew of Captain G. George as sailing master and navigator, his brother Harold and C. Bowman. They arrived at Kingston Bay, Norfolk Island on 27 December and departed for Auckland on 1 January arriving on 10 January after cruising down the North Auckland coast.

The second trans-Tasman race was sailed in 1934 and was again promoted by the Akarana Yacht Club. The event differed from the first race in that it was sailed from Auckland to Melbourne, not Sydney, a distance of 2624 km. Two yachts entered the race. They were a German-owned yawl visiting Auckland, *Te Rapunga*, and the Auckland 10.37 m cutter *Ngataki*.

Both yachts were well-known to local yachtsmen. *Ngataki* was built from timber milled from kauri logs found around the Hauraki Gulf, logs that had broken free from log rafts being towed from the Coromandel coast to Auckland. Her spars, rigging and canvas were all taken from the barque *Rewa*, which had been hulked at Hansen's Island, near Kawau. Her young owner and builder, John Wray, was to become a legend around the Pacific, and is today living on Waiheke Island.

The race started at 2.30 p.m. on 8 December 1934, both yachts racing for the Trans-tasman Cup and $140 prize money donated by the Victorian Yachting Association. *Ngataki* had a time allowance of 17 hours, and was crewed by John Wray as skipper-navigator, with a crew consisting of his brother Geoff Wray, M. Robinson and T. Graham. The *Te Rapunga* was crewed by Captain George Dibbern, Gunter Schramm (who had sailed with Captain Dibbern from Germany) and Aucklanders J. N. Tattersfield, Fred Norris and A. E. Vaile.

After an uneventful race *Te Rapunga* arrived at Melbourne on 27 December, with *Ngataki* arriving on 30 December. *Te Rapunga* won the cup and the prize money, and together with *Ngataki* returned to Auckland and continued her world voyage.

The third trans-Tasman race was from Auckland to Hobart, a distance of 2463 km. Two Auckland yachts, the scratch boat *Aurora Star* (a 12.2 m schooner) and *Wayfarer* (a 7.3 m canoe-stern cutter), with a time allowance of 44 hours, 37 minutes, three seconds, started at 7 p.m. on 18 January 1938. Neither were fated to reach Hobart. Clearing North Cape, both yachts were struck by a violent southerly gale which lasted four days. The *Wayfarer* hove-to, making water through a smashed skylight. She returned to Whangaroa on 26 January with a damaged rudder and in a leaking and battered condition.

The *Aurora Star* fared little better, being hove-to for 72 hours and drifting 640 km off course toward Lord Howe Island. They abandoned the race and put into the island under power. After a short stay the *Aurora Star* continued to Sydney, where she was sold.

World War II finished all ocean races, and it was 1948 before another trans-Tasman race was held. It was again organised by the Royal Akarana Yacht Club, now in conjunction with the Royal Prince Alfred Yacht Club of Sydney. This race was the first of several dominated by Australian yachts. In this event the winner was *Peer Gynt*, owned and sailed by the brothers T. and M. Halvorsen of Sydney.

The second post-war race across the Tasman from Auckland to Sydney started on 27 January 1951 and attracted the largest fleet of yachts yet to race across this stormy sea. From Auckland came the newly launched *Leda*, a 16.4 m cutter amateur-built by the Wilson brothers at Northcote aided by Jim Young, *Tara* (owned by Colin Wild), *White Squall*, *Hope* (both designed by Bert Woollacott) and *Rangi* which took part in the very first trans-Tasman race. Also in the fleet were *Sea Wolf*, a ketch from Whangarei, and two Sydney yachts — *Southern Maid* and *Solveig*, owned by the Halvorsen brothers.

The race was sailed in very light conditions, and *Leda* made history as the first ocean racing yacht to have daily newspapers delivered by aircraft. It all began on 30 January, the third day out, when the Auckland-to-Sydney TEAL (now Air New Zealand) Sunderland flying boat flew low over *Leda* and asked by radio if she wanted anything. The navigator on *Leda*, well-known yachtsman Terry Hammond, replied: "A new can-opener." Next day the flying boat banked low over *Leda* and dropped to her a can-opener wrapped in the morning newspaper. Each day they dropped the morning paper to *Leda*, much to the dismay of aviation officials when they later found out — it contravened aviation regulations. Never again will commercial aircraft drop newspapers to racing yachts.

Leda was first to finish, on 7 February, but the Halvorsens in *Solveig* won on handicap.

The trans-Tasman races continued a year later, in 1952, this time from Hobart to Auckland — a distance of 2463 km. The race was won by the ketch *Ladybird*, designed, built and owned by Bert Woollacott and sailed by his son John. His daughter Madge was in the crew, making it a real family effort. *Ladybird* covered the distance in 11 days, a fast passage for a yacht only 10 m overall. In 1954 an Auckland to Sydney race was sailed; it was won by the Christchurch ketch *Taihoa* owned and sailed by

experienced blue water yachtsman Neil Arrow.

The last official trans-Tasman race was held in 1961, when the Halvorsen brothers were again successful, this time in *Norla*. By now the trans-Tasman races were becoming less and less popular with both New Zealand and Australian yachtsmen. There have been several unofficial races since 1961, particularly among Auckland yachtsmen returning from Hobart after competing in the Sydney to Hobart classic, but the official races have ended.

It is not difficult to see why the race had lost appeal. The west to east crossing was usually a bash to windward all the way, in cold wet conditions, for 1932 km. For the same distance, in steady warm south-east tradewinds, the yachtsman could sail to warm tropic islands. In 1956

A tragic end to a fine ship. Historic photographs of the *Rangi*, a total loss at Cascades Bay, Norfolk Island in 1951. She was wrecked while returning to Auckland after competing in the 1951 race.

the Royal Akarana Yacht Club organised the first Auckland to Suva race, won as mentioned elsewhere by the Woollacott-designed and built cutter *Wanderer*.

The next ocean race to be organised was the Whangarei to Noumea race in 1964 — a new departure point and a new destination. And something else was now new in ocean racing. The yachts themselves had begun to change radically under the influence of the new Royal Ocean Racing Club (R.O.R.C.) of England regulations. Safety regulations were being tightened; gone was the free and easy attitude that prevailed in previous ocean races. Take the example of the cutter *Kismet* in the 1956 Suva race. She was owned and sailed by the colourful, "hard case" Aucklander Billy Patterson. Designed by Colin Wild, she was a sister ship of the well-known gulf cruisers *Valhalla* and *Valkyrie*. She was never intended for ocean racing. She had previously had her rig extended, which improved her performance, but as a result she was very tender. Billy Patterson knew this, and car-

ried sand bags hung from hooks in the windward deck beams to keep her upright. When she went about, the watch below moved the sandbags to the other deck beams — and so they sailed to Suva. Like newspapers being dropped from commercial airliners, this type of yacht will not be seen in ocean racing again.

The first of the new generation yachts which brought to New Zealand the R.O.R.C. influence was the Sparkman and Stephens *Cotton Blossom IV*, owned by Peter Spencer. This 12.2 m craft of radical appearance won virtually every race she entered, and pundits stated that she would kill coastal and ocean racing. However, as is so often the case, the radical design spurred others to beat her. The whole yacht racing scene was revitalised. Certainly the Woollacott type of yacht was completely outclassed and dropped out of the racing scene. The new yachts were more efficient, the rigs changed to R.O.R.C. rules. Mainsails became smaller, fore triangles grew, and masts moved to the centre of the boat to reduce pitching when punching to windward in conditions which would have forced the older boats to pack up and go home. Electronic sailing and navigating equipment began to make an appearance.

Above all, a new type of crewman began to emerge. He was a yachtsman who put yachting before everything. If an ocean race was on, his job was secondary. He was single, so social ties were no problem. But he did not have boat loyalty — one week one yacht, the next week perhaps a hot competitor. This attitude gave New Zealanders a hard driving, win-at-all-costs attitude which has made this country a name in world offshore racing.

The 1966 Auckland to Suva yacht race, organised by the Royal Akarana Yacht Club, attracted an entry of 37 yachts, ranging in size from 7.3 m to 18.6 m overall, all of which were handicapped under the R.O.R.C. rating rules. Ten years before, the 1956 Auckland to Suva race had only 13 entries, none longer than 10.3 m, a striking indication of the growth of ocean racing in 10 years. Yet on the day of the start — 30 April, 1966 — only 30 yachts faced the gun. Only 23 reached Suva, six returning and one sinking, the ill-fated *Tatariki*.

The great ocean racer *Fidelis*, hard on the wind with sails set to perfection, romping down the Auckland harbour.

Right: With nearly 280 sq m of sail set, *Fidelis* is really moving. Skipper Jim Davern crouches over the wheel to control her.

As expected, the cutter *Fidelis*, sailed by Jim Davern, with an elapsed time of nine days, 12 hours, 50 minutes and 36 seconds, was first to finish — although on corrected time she finished 14th overall. A long skinny type of boat, *Fidelis* was never considered suitable for ocean racing. Blue water yachtsmen, used to short ends, said her long overhangs would break off in a sizable sea and her high aspect ratio rig would collapse over the side. Jim Davern proved them wrong.

Fidelis measures 18.6 m overall, 14.6 m on the waterline, 3 m in beam, with a 2.3 m draught. She displaces 12.2 tonnes and has a working sail area of 120 sq m. *Fidelis* was designed by Vic Speight (who had previously owned the old Logan-built *Iorangi*). She was based on a 75 sq m design by Knud Reimers of Sweden — the same design on which the Tercel brothers had based the design of *Ranger*. She was built by

Fred and Jim Lidgard (both later lost off North Cape) at Bayswater.

Fidelis proved a disappointment when first launched in 1959. Jim Davern, who had previously owned the Stewart 34 *Princess*, bought her in 1964, and after many modifications to the rig and rudder finally got her to perform. The Suva race was the first ocean passage for *Fidelis*, and the only mishap she suffered was the loss of a spade rudder two days out when the 57 mm solid tobin bronze shaft sheared while she was reaching at 10 knots under double reefed main and storm jib. The old stock rudder, which was still fitted and used as a trim tab, was pressed into service, and after 10

Fidelis again. Davern sails his big champion down Sydney Harbour on yet another Sydney to Hobart race while his crew look out for spectator boats, always a hazard at the start of this great event. *Fidelis* won this race, in 1967.

This shot of *Fidelis* hard on the wind on the port tack with the crew lining the windward deck shows the easy entry and clean wake of this offshore flier.

minutes delay *Fidelis* continued racing to Suva.

The overall winner of this eventful race was *Roulette*, owned and sailed by Fred Andrews, with a young Chris Bouzaid in the crew. The 9.3 m *Roulette* was designed by Jack Brooke. The Robb-designed yawl *Aronui*, sailed by Ray Walker was second, and *Tiare Moana*, a 9.4 m sloop designed by John Lidgard, was third.

In April 1967 the Onerahi Yacht Club held another Whangarei to Noumea Race. This race was notable for the entry of the *Rainbow II*, launched only 14 days earlier. The race was sailed in a fresh southerly air-stream, and the first yacht to finish was the *Fidelis*. *Rainbow II* averaged seven knots for the 1932 km to beat *Fidelis* on corrected time by one and a half hours.

Other ocean races followed. The first single-handed trans-Tasman race, from New Plymouth to Mooloolaba in Queensland, attracted an entry of five yachts. These were the 10.67 m Piver-designed trimaran *Rebel*, sailed by American Marvin Glenn, the John Spencer-designed *Tom Bowline*, sailed by Don Boyes-Barnes, the *Mirrool*, a 9 m fibreglass Australian Clansman design sailed by Charles Ure, *Kochab II*, a Robb-designed 16 m yacht sailed by 20-year-old Whangarei boatbuilding apprentice Noel Barrott, and *Kitiga*, a 6.4 m bilge keeler sailed by Kerikeri orchardist Jerry Clark (who holds a master mariner's ticket). After a fair weather race *Rebel* finished first, sailing the 2095 km in just over nine days.

Although not a New Zealand race, the 1970 Sydney to Hobart race attracted a great deal of interest in this country because of the entry of the new and still-to-be-tuned *Buccaneer*. Only one other New Zealand entrant was in the race, the 10.2 m *Prospector* from Lyttelton. This 1970 race was the first to be sailed under the new I.O.R. rules and was considered to be the toughest in the race's 26-year history. *Buccaneer* finished in three days, 14 hours, 16 minutes — 11 hours behind *Ondine's* 1962 record. Handicap winner was *Pacha* from New South Wales, but *Buccaneer's* performance greatly pleased designer John Spencer.

There was another Auckland to Suva yacht race in May 1973, which attracted a then record race fleet of 80 yachts. Weather conditions proved very favourable; the prevailing trade winds blew a steady 25 to 30 knots, which pushed the big fleet to Suva in record time. The Auckland sloop *Ta'Aroa*, designed by Olin Stephens and owned by Doug Bremner, was first home in a record time of five days, 12 hours, 52 minutes, cutting over 48 hours from the previous fastest time, held by the big cutter *Kahurangi*.

Designed by Arthur Robb and owned for many years by Lawrence Nathan, *Kahurangi*

measures 18.9 m overall, 12.7 m on the waterline, with a beam of 3.7 m and a draught of 3.2 m. She displaces 20.3 tonnes and is constructed traditionally of three-skin diagonal heart kauri. *Kahurangi* was launched on 20 November 1952 from the yard of Percy Voss, who made an excellent job of her construction. Rigged as a Bermuda cutter and carrying 134 sq m of sail, *Kahurangi* has for many years competed with much success in the Auckland first division keeler fleet in both inshore and offshore races. At the time of writing *Kahurangi* is being prepared for a cruise to the Mediterranean via the Panama Canal. This will realise a life-long ambition of owner Lawrence Nathan to sail the waters of the Greek Islands and the pleasure resorts of the French coast.

A busy year for ocean racing was 1974. The year started with an unofficial race from Hobart to Auckland for New Zealand yachts that had

The powerful *Buccaneer* reaches up Hobart's Derwent River to finish first in the 1971 Sydney to Hobart ocean classic.

The foredeck crew at work on the Sparkman and Stephens-designed *Ta-Aroa*, owned by Doug Bremner. This photograph shows the complexity and sheer size of the gear carried on these big keelers. Look at the size of the spinnaker boom here being hoisted up the mast prior to the spinnaker itself being hoisted.

competed in the 1973 Sydney to Hobart race, the last of the Southern Cross Cup series. The race was won on corrected time by *Quicksilver*, owned and built by the late Brin Wilson, but sailed by his son Richard. She beat the *Inca*, owned by Evan Julian but sailed by Allan Bell, by only 28 seconds — after racing nearly 2250 km.

This 1973 Southern Cross Cup challenge by the New Zealand team of *Inca*, *Barnacle Bill* (owned and sailed by Doug Johnstone) and *Quicksilver* was regarded as a preliminary for

the 1975 Admiral's Cup challenge in England. After the three short races in and around Sydney Harbour the New Zealand team had a 57-point lead over the British team, with Hong Kong and New South Wales following. But five hours after the start of the 1014 km classic race to Hobart, tragedy struck. A crewman on *Inca*, John Sarney, only 20 years old, collapsed and died. *Inca* lost seven and a half hours going into Jervis Bay, where the body was put ashore. *Inca* eventually finished in 63rd place (*Barnacle Bill* was 12th and *Quicksilver* 22nd), and New Zealand finished second in the Southern Cross Cup, 51 points behind the British team.

Inca, *Barnacle Bill* and *Gerontius* went on to represent New Zealand in the Admiral's Cup series in August 1975.

The weather for the four-race series, held in

the English Channel, with the race headquarters at Cowes on the Isle of Wight, was sadly to the detriment of the New Zealand team. For once in a lifetime the British weather was so hot that the famous sou'-westerly depression experienced in previous contests was blocked off by a series of highs. The series was sailed not in thrashing, rain-laden winds, but in heat hazes and light zephyrs! The weather situation was not helped by the strongest tidal streams of the whole year.

The light winds and strong tides conspired to make the 1975 Admiral's Cup contest a series for small, light boats. The outdated and heavy *Inca* and *Barnacle Bill* just were not competitive. The skippering and crew work generally was also under the standard of the leading teams. *Inca*

was disqualified from the vital fourth race, the famous 970 km Fastnet race being sailed for the 50th year, only 10 minutes after the start for a simple port and starboard incident with the Swedish yacht *Attaque*. *Gerontius* showed signs at times of her potential, but a lack of strong fair winds to drive her dinghy-like hull prevented a race-winning performance.

The New Zealand team was grimly determined and well prepared. With outdated yachts and little top line competition behind them, their final fifth overall placing with 684 points in a record entry of 19 teams was a creditable performance. The winning British team had the benefit of local knowledge of the tricky sailing conditions, and took the cup for the sixth time in the 10-year history of the series.

The last yacht Brin Wilson owned. *Quicksilver* beats up the river to Hobart during the 1973 Southern Cross series.

A magnificent action shot of the great offshore racer *Kahurangi*, designed by Arthur Robb and launched in 1952. Here she runs at speed with spinnaker set. She has proved a most successful ocean racer.

Meanwhile the Banks Peninsula Cruising Club's Auckland to Lyttelton race, the longest domestic ocean race in New Zealand, had started on 12 January 1974 and attracted an entry of 19 yachts (including three multi-hulls). The race was sailed in light, frustrating conditions, and the worst problem experienced was — of all things — collisions with whales. The Christchurch trimaran *Rebel II* (owned by Tony Allan) was forced to retire after losing her rudder in this fashion. *Kochab II* (owned by Tom Nesbit) suffered the same problem — but managed to finish — when they hit the big mammals off the Kaikoura coast.

First to finish was *Buccaneer*, but the one-tonners dominated the corrected times. *Escapade*, owned by Gil Hedges but chartered by Don St. Clair Brown, took overall place, with *Wai-Aniwa* (Chris Bouzaid) second and *Pathfinder* (Ian Titchener) third. *Pathfinder* actually beat *Wai-Aniwa* across the line but was placed third because of the age allowance claimed by *Wai-Aniwa*.

In May 1974 another inaugural ocean race took place. This was the Auckland to Rarotonga race, organised jointly by the Rarotonga Sailing Club and the Royal New Zealand Yacht Squadron. The race started off Orakei Wharf on Saturday 4 May. First to finish was *Kahurangi*, which took nine days, six hours and 14 minutes for the passage, followed by *Charlemagne*, *Totolo* and *Roulette II*. On the R.N.Z.Y.S. time correction system *Charlemagne* was first, *Sirius* second and *Roulette II* third. The I.O.R. rating result was *Roulette II* first, *Kahurangi* second, *Charlemagne* third.

Sailed virtually in conjunction with the Rarotonga race was the second New Plymouth to

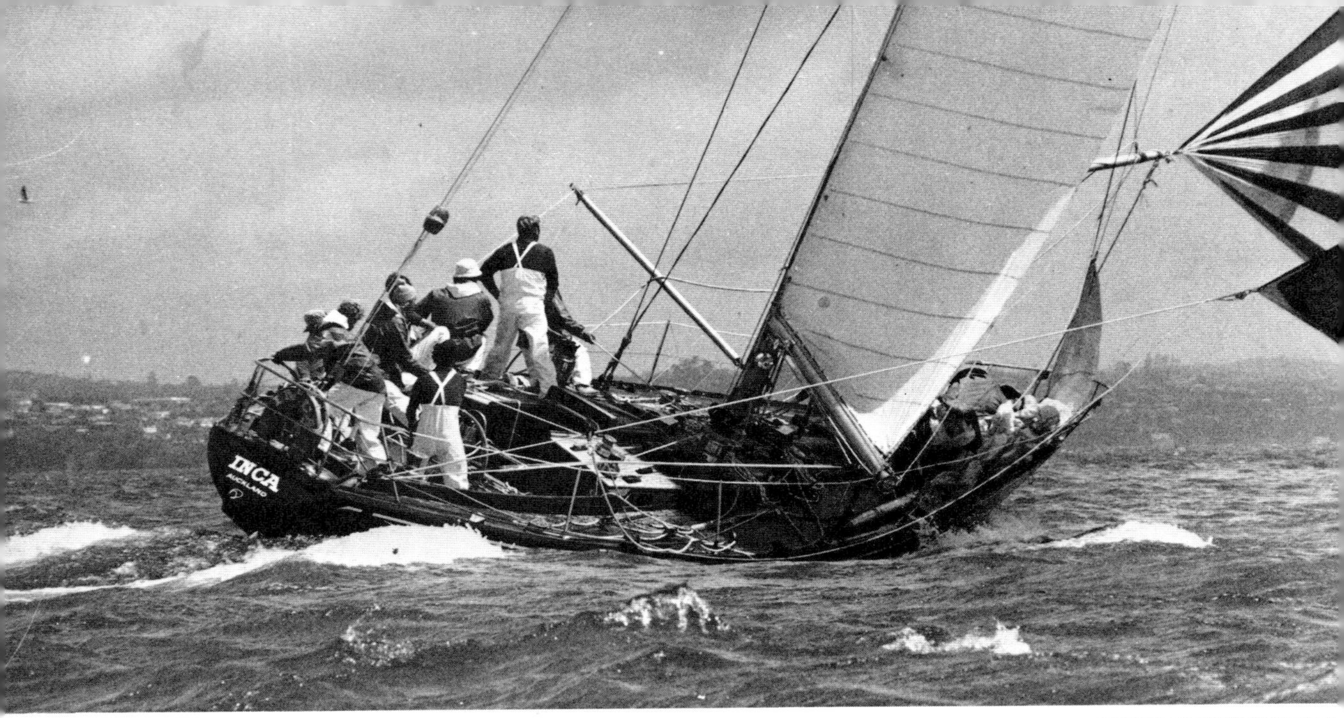
INCA
AUCKLAND
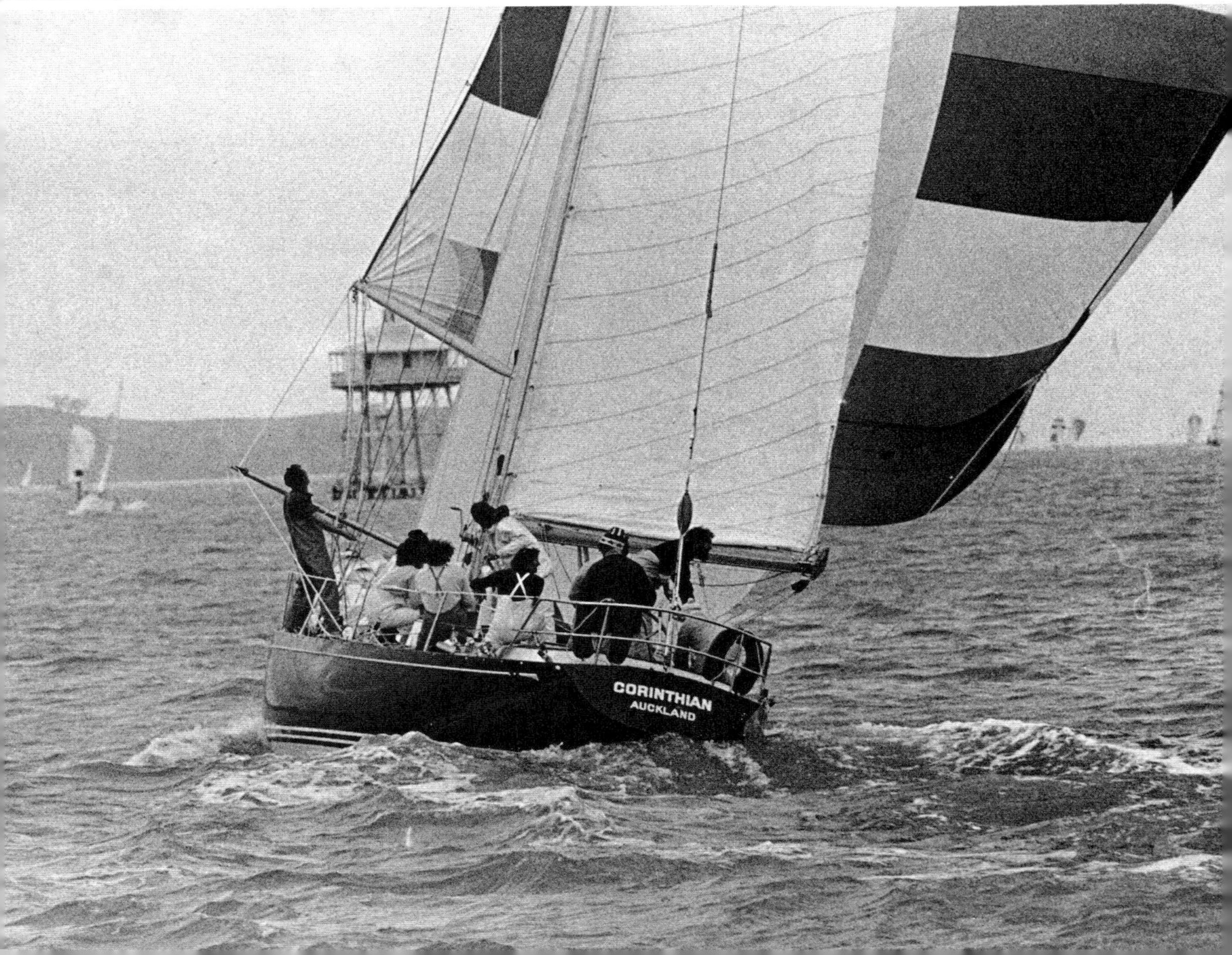
CORINTHIAN
AUCKLAND

Fine shots of New Zealand Admiral's Cup yachts in action during trials to select the 1975 Admiral's Cup team. Left: *Inca*, all power as she reaches down the Rangitoto Channel with her crew alert for any wind changes. Below left: the Sparkman and Stephens-designed *Corinthian*, owned by Russ Hooper; she did not make the New Zealand team. Right: *Barnacle Bill*, owned at the time of his death by former All Black Ron Jarden. Below: *Gerontius*, designed by Bruce Farr, slogging it out on Auckland harbour.

Mooloolaba trans-Tasman single-handed race, which started on 27 April 1974. Ten entries were received, ranging in size from the trimaran *Rebel II* to the 5.79 m ferro-cement sloop *Roc*. The race was also notable for the first entry of a woman in a single-handed race. She was Annette Wilde who sailed the 10 m ferro-cement sloop *Valya*. A condition of entry was that each contestant had to sail a 805 km single handed passage to qualify. The first yacht to finish the 2090 km course was the 7.3 m fibreglass sloop *Raha*, sailed by Bill Belcher, closely followed by the favourites *Carmita*, a 9 m sloop sailed by Pony Moore, and *Rebel II*. John Mansell, who was later to sail in the 1976 Atlantic solo race in his 8.5 m cutter *Innovator*, was fourth.

The next ocean race was the Whangarei to Noumea race, which started on 19 April 1975. It was organised jointly by the Onerahi Yacht Club and Cercle Nautique Caledonian Yacht Club. Many of the top New Zealand ocean racing yachts such as *Buccaneer*, who was first to finish, followed by *Ta'aroa*, *Quando*, *Kailua* and *Volante*, competed in a race expected to be a fast downhill ride under spinnaker all the way. But the race proved to be a fickle affair plagued by variable breezes, which frustrated skippers and crews. The fleet was divided into five divisions, and on the I.O.R. rating the overall winner was the little-fancied Cavalier half-tonner *Cochrane*,

owned and sailed by Doug Dick. *Trauma*, sailed by Mark Williams, was second with *Kishmul*, Richard Tapper and Lester Smith, third.

The following year, 1976, saw yet another new ocean race — from Tauranga to Vila in the New Hebrides, a distance of 2415 km. It attracted an entry of 15 yachts, ranging in size from the 16.4 m Allan Mummery-designed *Freedom of Leigh*, owned and sailed by Reg Thomas, to the 9.4 m John Lidgard-designed *Demijohn*, skippered by the very experienced Jack Allen. Three other yachts were designed by John Lidgard — *Trauma*, *Pemerquable* and *Spero*. The overall winner was *Demijohn*, which also had the designer on board. This yacht also took first place in the B-division. The winner of the A-division was *Snow White*, designed by Laurie Davidson and owned and sailed by Bob Graham.

The attraction of ocean racing can only be understood by those who have participated. The broken sleep, the cold, the sometimes frightening conditions, all build a brotherhood between crew members, for each man or woman (for the female sex are today ocean racing in ever increasing numbers) depends on the other to get their little ship to its destination. Once they have arrived, the hardships (and the seasickness) are forgotten as experiences are swapped with crews off competing yachts. Ocean racing is one of the last man-against-nature challenges in the world. It attracts the sort of person who wants more from life than the 8 a.m. to 5 p.m. commuter grind and staid suburban living.

John Mansell's *Innovator*, fourth in the 1974 trans-Tasman singlehanded race, here preparing in New Plymouth for the start of the race.

Above: *Buccaneer* and *Sirius* (A.67) jockeying for position at the start of the 1975 Whangarei to Noumea ocean race.

Below: The Bob Miller-designed *Volante* chases *Fidelis* down the side of Rangitoto.

Epilogue

DURING THE MONTHS of research necessary to record accurately the development of New Zealand yachting since the middle of last century, it became more and more obvious that the development of this great sport has followed a series of cycles. On closer examination this trend has been invariably tied to one factor — money.

Since the days of the seventeenth century when the English kings had "pleasure yachts" built (monsters by today's standards) yachting has been the sport of the wealthy. One hundred and thirty years ago the yachts of Auckland and Wellington (the two major yachting centres) were owned by the importers and merchants, men who realised that the young country needed goods for development, and thus grew rich by supplying them.

As the country grew and prospered into the 1880s so did the sport. Boatbuilders like Charles Bailey Senior, Robert Logan Senior, George Niccol and Alex Alison could not build yachts fast enough to meet the demand from prospective owners. The discovery of gold, particularly in the Thames and Otago fields, created extremely wealthy men overnight, men who wanted a yacht — primarily for social reasons, but these yachts were invariably raced (usually for a wager with another wealthy owner) by sailing masters and paid crews.

It can be claimed that during the 20 years between 1870 and 1890 the yachtbuilding industry provided New Zealand's first manufactured exports. The well-built New Zealand yachts, fast and seaworthy, had created a name and Australian, South African and even American owners wanted such yachts to beat locally built boats.

The yachts at this time were long, deep, narrow and slack-bilged, with enormous gaff rigs. They were scathingly referred to as "lead-mines" or "planks on edges". They were "wet" and hard to sail, needing large crews. The design of these yachts was based on the English boats, which had been developed for the short, sharp seas and strong tides found around the British coast. Gradually the New Zealand design form changed, until in the 1890s the fin keel "skim dishes" were evolved. The pendulum then swung too far — these "fin and bulb" keelers were cranky and difficult to sail.

It was not until the Scottish genius George Watson designed the new, radical, king's yacht *Britannia*, with her spoon bow, powerful mid-section, and long run aft, which proved so successful, that yacht design stabilised. New Zealand designers and builders, notably the Logan brothers, were quick to follow Watson's lead. This style of yacht, so well demonstrated by the powerful *Ariki* and *Rainbow* was to stay with us until the late 1950s. Then John Spencer — catering primarily to the amateur builder and incorporating technological advances in marine plywood and greatly improved glues — dramatically changed the shape of yachts. The light displacement trend was also followed by international designers such as Sparkman and Stephens, who during the 1960s completely dominated the design of offshore and rating class yachts. Today, in the middle of the 1970s, they in turn have been displaced by young local designers such as Bruce Farr and Paul Whiting and, overseas, Doug Peterson and Ron Holland.

However the economic climate (that is, money) still determines the level of yachting activity in New Zealand. As the country recovered from the depression of the 1890s, the yachtbuilding industry was busy in the first decade of this century. Again, after World War I through the 1920s the industry thrived; but in the 1930s, with the Great Depression, virtually no new large racing yachts were built. Indeed, from the middle 1920s, when the cutters *Prize* and *Ngatoa* were launched, no major yacht was built until the late 1930s — when such yachts as *Little Jim*, *Tawera* and *Matia* took to the water.

The 1940s were affected by World War II, and few large keelers were built until the middle 1950s. Then the boom occurred, and the 20 years to the present day has seen a flood of yacht-building. In fact it has been said that in Auckland one pleasure boat (including launches) over 9 m in length is launched every day. This tremendous growth of the pleasure boat fleet has strained resources. Marinas, a recent development, are full. Waiting lists have been closed. Protected moorings are full to capacity, and unprotected areas of the Auckland harbour such as that off Northcote Point have 130 to 140 boats moored where even 10 years ago there would be just one or two boats.

Water pollution is a serious problem around the more popular Hauraki Gulf anchorages, and authorities are considering requiring all pleasure craft to have holding tanks for sewage to prevent such pollution. What has happened is similar to that experienced overseas (for the problem occurs not only in New Zealand) in that the number of pleasure boats greatly exceeds the facilities, both natural and man made, available to handle them.

However there are signs that the number of pleasure boats being built is abating as the economic situation of the country becomes less buoyant. This will give a breathing space to enable the man-made facilities to catch up with the demand.

The 1975 Admiral's Cup challenge in England was a valuable lesson in which we learnt that a country of three million people cannot compete on an equal basis with the far larger, wealthier industrialised countries of the Northern Hemisphere. We can offer enthusiasm, skill and dedication, but to reach the top in such competition — and to stay there — requires the very best of machinery. In the Admiral's Cup challenge, the yachts we thought were competitive were in fact outdated. It would appear that in New Zealand our forte in international yachting is the centreboard one-design classes — where great yachtsmen like the late Clive Roberts did so much for this country — and the level rating classes, quarter, half and even one-ton, where human attributes are still more important than the money spent on hull, rigging and sails.

Looking ahead, it is not difficult to see that the traditional New Zealand construction methods using heart kauri planking, or three-diagonal skins, is virtually finished. This has been bought about by two factors; firstly the very limited supply of kauri and its associated high price, and secondly the high cost and lack of skilled labour available to build such yachts. What has replaced this construction method is the mass-produced stock boat, built of fibreglass and popped out of a mould. This relatively low cost building method has aggravated the problem of overcrowded moorings and pollution in that it has put the ownership of pleasure boats within the reach of people who in past years just could not afford such a boat unless they built it themselves. Yet why should yachting be confined to just the wealthy, as in past years? The thrill of running free under spinnaker in sunny sparkling waters, or thrashing to windward, belongs to everyone. It is hoped it will always be this way.

Index

OTHER SAILING AND BOATING BOOKS FROM REEDS

Trailer-Sailers by Jeff Toghill

Trailer-sailers are rapidly gaining popularity and Jeff Toghill provides an invaluable guide to both prospective and current owners of these versatile craft.

The Yachtsman's Navigation Manual by Jeff Toghill

Every aspect of accurate navigation is covered in this simply and clearly written book, including advice for ocean-going yachtsmen. Fully illustrated.

Sailing for Beginners by Jeff Toghill

All that the new yachtsman needs to know, as well as much useful information for the experienced yachtsman.

Power Boating by Jeff Toghill

This book aims to help power boat owners solve problems that can prevent full enjoyment of boating. Invaluable information and advice.

The Boat Owner's Maintenance Manual by Jeff Toghill

A comprehensive volume covering all aspects of maintenance and repair of yachts, from sailing dinghies to keelers.

Coastal Navigation for Beginners by Jeff Toghill

Using a step-by-step approach the various aspects of navigating in small boats are covered in full. An ideal first handbook.